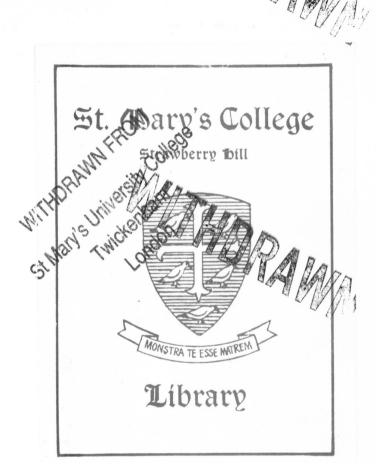

SHADOWS
OF
HEAVEN

SHADOWS OF HEAVEN

Religion and Fantasy
in the Writing of
C. S. Lewis,
Charles Williams,
and J. R. R. Tolkien

Gunnar Urang

SCM PRESS LTD

334 01497 2

First British edition 1971
published by SCM Press Ltd
56 Bloomsbury Street London WC1

© United Church Press 1971

Typeset in the United States of America
Printed in Great Britain by
Lowe & Brydone (Printers) Ltd., London

TABLE OF CONTENTS

vii **ACKNOWLEDGMENTS**

1 **INTRODUCTION**

5 **CHAPTER 1 C. S. Lewis:**
Fantasy and the Metaphysics of Faith

51 **CHAPTER 2 Charles Williams:**
Fantasy and the Ontology of Love

93 **CHAPTER 3 J. R. R. Tolkien:**
Fantasy and the Phenomenology of Hope

131 **CHAPTER 4 Conclusion:**
Fantasy and the "Motions of Grace"

171 **NOTES**

                                    Yet for thy good
This is dispensed, and what surmounts the reach
Of human sense I shall delineate so,
By likening spiritual to corporal forms,
As may express them best, though what if Earth
Be but the shadow of Heaven, and things therein
Each to other like, more than on Earth is thought?

—*Paradise Lost,* V, 570–76

ACKNOWLEDGMENTS

English publishers of the main works of Lewis, Williams and Tolkien, to whom we are grateful for permission to use the extracts illustrating the text, are:

C. S. Lewis

Geoffrey Bles: *The Pilgrim's Regress*, 1933
The Problem of Pain, 1940
Christian Behaviour, 1943
Beyond Personality, 1944
The Great Divorce, 1945
Miracles, 1947
Surprised by Joy, 1955
Till We Have Faces, 1956
The Screwtape Letters and *Screwtape Proposes a Toast*, 1961
Letters to Malcolm, 1964
Poems ed. Walter Hooper, 1964

The Bodley Head: *Out of the Silent Planet*, n.e. 1945
Perelandra, 1943
That Hideous Strength, 1945

Charles Williams

Faber & Faber: *All Hallows Eve*, 2e 1945
War in Heaven, 2e 1947
Many Dimensions, 2e 1947
Descant of the Dove, 2e 1950
He Came Down from Heaven and *Forgiveness of Sin*, 1950
The Place of the Lion, 2e 1952
The Greater Trumps, 2e 1954
Shadows of Ecstasy, 1965

OUP: *Collected Plays*, 1963

J. R. R. Tolkien

George Allen & Unwin: *The Lord of the Rings*, 3 vols, 2e 1966

English publishers of other important books referred to in the notes are:

Jocelyn Gibb (ed), *Light on C. S. Lewis*, Geoffrey Bles 1965
C. S. Lewis (ed), *Essays Presented to Charles Williams*, OUP 1947
W. H. Lewis (ed), *Letters of C. S. Lewis*, Geoffrey Bles 1966
Anne Ridler (ed), Charles Williams, *The image of the city and Other Essays*, OUP 1958

INTRODUCTION

At the outbreak of war in September 1939, Oxford University Press was evacuated from London to Southfield House in Oxford. Among the evacuees was Charles Williams, who had been with the press since 1908. The Williams who arrived in Oxford was fifty-three years old and, though not a university man, was well known as a lecturer, essayist, playwright, novelist, and poet.

But the men whose circle he became a part of in Oxford were university men indeed. The "Inklings," as they called themselves, were in the habit of meeting weekly—occasionally twice in a week—either in C. S. Lewis' rooms at Magdalen or at some nearby pub, usually to hear and to discuss something that one of their number had written. At various times the group included A. H. Dyson, Owen Barfield, W. H. Lewis, and Gervase Mathew, as well as better-known members: J. R. R. Tolkien and C. S. Lewis. Lewis and Tolkien had at that time been friends for a number of years. At the time of Charles Williams' arrival Tolkien was forty-seven years old, had been at Oxford for fourteen years, and was known outside the university for two things: his scholarly and critical work in Old and Middle English literature and his fantasy for children, *The Hobbit*. C. S. Lewis, another Oxford don, somewhat younger than both Williams and Tolkien, had gained his reputation mainly for the scholarly study *The Allegory of Love* and the popular space fantasy *Out of the Silent Planet*. Lewis and Williams had already become acquainted, Lewis having been impressed by Williams' fantasy *The Place of the Lion* and Williams having enthusiastically welcomed *The Allegory of Love*.[1]

The three can clearly be regarded, then, as a "group." They were allied not only by friendship but by scholarly and critical interests, concerning themselves primarily with the literature of the Middle Ages and more generally with the tradition of what might be called Christian transcendentalism in poetry (Spenser, Milton, Wordsworth, Coleridge, Patmore). They shared a lively concern for theology, although only Williams and Lewis actually produced lay theology. Finally—and of most relevance to the subject of this book—they all wrote fantasy.

In recent years a growing interest in literary fantasy—of which the Tolkien fad of the sixties is only one, though perhaps the most impressive, manifestation—has been paralleled by a new and more disciplined study of the techniques of fiction. One concept which this criticism has been reexamining—particularly in the context of the modern symbolic novel but also, inevitably, in relation to fantasy—is that of allegory. This involves a questioning of the pejorative use of the term in much of the "New Criticism," particularly insofar as that critical school has been under the spell of Coleridge, who associated allegory with the mechanical activity of the fancy rather than the organic life of the imagination. It also brings with it a rethinking of the related concept of myth and even of the basic notion of the literary symbol.[2]

But to rethink these terms is to raise once again the question of belief. And it is significant that while this reexamination of allegory and symbol has been in progress, other critics have been asking their questions about the place of belief, or vision, in literary creation and discovery.[3] In general, such critics would subscribe to Martin Jarrett-Kerr's assertion that

> since man is a whole, his basic attitudes to life, his "ultimate pre-suppositions," and therefore his beliefs, run into his behavior (public and private) at one point, into his imagination and his dreams at another, and so at yet another into his language, imagery and (if he is a poet) versification.[4]

In light of these developments the literary fantasy of Lewis, Williams, and Tolkien is of particular interest. In each of their works, first of all, the idea of the form seems to be correlated with a pattern of believed ideas, so that one would be inclined to call the fantasy allegorical; at the same time, however, these writers want very much to insist that they are writing not allegory but "myth." Furthermore, the ideas which seem to govern the structure often belong to precisely that orthodoxy which has been radically called into question by the modern intellect and sensibility. All three writers, finally, have not only written fantasy but have written *about* fantasy—about the theory and technique of literary fantasy and about the religious beliefs which inform their kind of fantasy.

Accordingly, a study such as this must ask two large questions. First, how does the shape of each writer's belief correlate with the unique literary qualities of his fiction? This descriptive task is my concern in the first three chapters; each deals inductively with the prose fantasy of one author in the group and moves toward a tentative assessment of his work, seeking to measure its effectiveness in relation to the norms implied by the work itself. The concluding chapter attempts to pose a larger question. In light of certain prevailing weaknesses in this body of work—even in light of the general tendency of the ideas embodied therein—can the pattern of belief represented by the work be considered adequate to the experience and the developing consciousness of modern man?

A critical approach adequate to these undertakings will move, it seems to me, along lines close to those suggested by Derek Savage. "As the novelist presents life to itself as art," Savage argues, so the critic's work is "to present art to itself as thought," to draw out the concealed meanings, to trace them all to their common center, and to relate them to the general cultural situation.[5] One can begin, then, with a kind of literary equivalent to what would be, for the philosopher, phenomenological analysis. For literature, as Hillis Miller reminds us, is a form of consciousness, and literary criticism is the analysis of this form in all its varieties. But consciousness is always consciousness *of* something. Thus we must add that "a work of literature is the act whereby a mind takes possession of space, time, nature, or other minds." The critic's endeavor must be "to identify himself with the subjectivity expressed in the words, to relive that life from the inside, and to constitute it anew in his criticism."[6] In attempting that task I have found that the inner life of these fantasies throbs with the idea of divine grace—more specifically, with the three manifestations of grace traditionally called faith, hope, and love, and more specifically still, with the possibility of grace for the modern mind. Can faith, hope, and love be made available to that sensibility which has been corroded by the acids of modernity? The part that fantasy plays in this literary-theological project is the theme of the first three chapters.

But there is another tradition in modern criticism—including such disparate figures as D. H. Lawrence, F. O. Matthiessen, Lionel Trilling, and Raymond Williams—in which the critic accepts a broader responsibility toward his culture, in which he considers the work—and not merely descriptively—in relation to the general cultural situation. The final chapter moves in this direction. My purpose is not, of course, to decide whether a particular author is pernicious or healthful, according to some ideological criterion; criticism must be more dialectical than that. But literary criticism must be a social act; one's concern is not just to grasp the aesthetic terms in which, within the work, the existential question is put but also to challenge the adequacy of the terms themselves, as well as any synthesis toward which they may point. The concluding chapter seeks to judge, then, the extent to which the kind of fantasy written by Lewis, Williams, and Tolkien presents a cogent interpretation of those "motions of grace" which would appear to be felt along the pulses of the people of our age.

In writing this book I have incurred debts of gratitude to several persons, notably to my friend Prof. Burton Cooper and to my advisor and friend Nathan Scott. Burton Cooper's influence is evident particularly in the theological analysis of the last chapter. Nathan Scott's encouragement and advice is reflected in every page—and even in the conception of the project as a whole, since it was a suggestion from him which set it in motion.

C. S. LEWIS: FANTASY AND THE METAPHYSICS OF FAITH

CHAPTER 1

The fantasy of C. S. Lewis, taken as a whole, begins in autobiography, moves into apologetics, and then returns—but with a difference—to autobiography. The fiction for which he is best known was published between 1938 and 1945, almost precisely in the middle of his career as a writer. These books—*Out of the Silent Planet, Perelandra,* and *That Hideous Strength* (the so-called space trilogy), along with *The Screwtape Letters* and *The Great Divorce* —function in part as implicit apologetic, as a defense of the Christian faith, which takes particular account of the skepticism or hostility of the nonbeliever. (Much of Lewis' explicitly apologetic writing, his lay theology, also dates from this period, the most important books appearing between 1940 and 1947.[1]) For most readers of C. S. Lewis, autobiography means his *Surprised by Joy: The Shape of My Early Life* (1955). But the first of his "autobiographies" had appeared almost thirty years earlier in the form of a fantasy, a narrative poem in nine cantos called *Dymer* (1926). *The Pilgrim's Regress* (1933) brought that story up to date and retold it in the light of Lewis' conversion to Christianity. It also moved beyond symbolic autobiography, announcing itself—by way of its subtitle—as "An Allegorical Apology for Christianity, Reason, and Romanticism." *Till We Have Faces* (1956), the last published fiction by C. S. Lewis, manifests a similiar apologetic intention. But in that book— perhaps because the idea for it had "lived in the author's mind, thickening and hardening with the years, ever since he was an undergraduate"—Lewis also reverted to spiritual autobiography.

The term regress notwithstanding, *The Pilgrim's Regress*[2] is, like Bunyan's "progress," an allegorical journey "from this world to that which is to come," from immersion in this-worldly values to a full recognition of the claims of the other world and of the relation between the two worlds. In this it is like *Till We Have Faces* and unlike the fantasies in between, which embody primarily the other great allegorical theme of the struggle *between* the two worlds, the "holy war" for "Mansoul." In *The Pilgrim's Regress* C. S. Lewis (like Bunyan before him and like Saint Augustine before both of them) writes as an adult convert to Christianity, examining his past in order to understand for himself and make known to others how he has become what he now is. Just as John Bunyan in his earlier years had fed his imagination on popular tales of knights and giants and dragons, so Lewis' memory is filled with the fantasies of George Macdonald, William Morris, and H. G. Wells.

Out of such spiritual experience and such images of fantasy both Bunyan and Lewis build allegory. Each establishes the fantastic character of his fictional world by means of the dream framework, which is one way of emphasizing what all allegory implies: that what we receive from the work is not mirror images of reality, but images projected to suggest the motions of the "inner" life. The pattern of action in each book reinforces the effect brought about by the dream framework, even as that framework makes "probable" the events of the story. It is the arbitrary—free and yet bound— world of dreams, with its mysterious personages, its commands and prohibitions, and its symbolic topography. In both books these personages and places, symbolically named, and these commands and prohibitions, explained in long expository passages, carry the burden of the allegorical meaning.

Certain differences, of course, become equally obvious. Some of these differences between the adventures of the two pilgrims may be accounted for theologically. As Dorothy Sayers has pointed out, the advent of Calvinism brought one of those profound changes in psychological outlook which tend to be productive of allegory as a literary fashion. It "transferred the sensitive area of religious experience from confrontation with a transcendent God without, to the workings of the Spirit within the Soul."[3] Thus Bunyan's concern is with the sense of moral guilt and helplessness and the need of forgiveness and power; and the means for this are all religious, consisting of the Bible, preaching and teaching, prayer, and Christian companionship. C. S. Lewis, however, stands in the Catholic tradition. Created nature can enlist the interest of the natural man in a way that is not necessarily idolatrous but potentially gracious. Supernatural grace must supervene, however, to reveal the true meaning of the desire and to reorient it. His is also a "Romantic," an aesthetic rather than a rationalistic, way; for this natural experience is associated for him with inanimate nature and the literature of the marvelous, and consists in an intense longing which no object of desire can satisfy. "It appeared to me," he writes in the preface to the third edition of *The Pilgrim's Regress,*

> that if a man diligently followed this desire, pursuing the false objects until their falsity appeared and then resolutely abandoning them, he must come out at last into the clear knowledge that the human soul was made to enjoy some object that is never fully given . . . in our present mode of subjective and spatio-temporal experience. . . . The dialectic of Desire, faithfully followed, would retrieve all mistakes, head you off from all false paths, and force you not to propound, but to live through, a sort of ontological proof.[4]

Bunyan's Christian is an adult. But Lewis, convinced of "the real *praeparatio evangelica* inherent in certain immediately sub-Christian experiences,"[5] begins his story with events that take place during the childhood of a boy called John, who lives in Puritania and sets out for the mysterious island of Sweet Desire. For similar reasons, Lewis' work is an apology not only for Christianity but also for "Reason" and "Romanticism."

Other differences arise out of the peculiarities of the path toward conversion which each man followed. Lewis says of his way: "It is a road very rarely trodden"; Bunyan's was, in his day at least, a more typical conversion. The times make a difference too. C. S. Lewis is very conscious of writing for an audience which does not share the presuppositions that have become his as a convert. Thus he must bring to life allegorically not only the hindrances and helps in the way, but also the intimations or "inklings" that have drawn him toward belief. For both endeavors he enlists the aid of fantasy.

Because so many of the stumbling blocks are associated, for Lewis, with intellectual concepts or ideologies and because he feels many of these to be merely unfortunate fads, much of his fantasy carries out a satirical function, occasionally degenerating into invective. At other times it serves to intimate the beauty and desirability of what is ideal or ultimate, often in passages of "heightened" prose which are singularly unsuccessful.

But Lewis himself came to acknowledge this early work as defective; and I have spent this much time on it primarily in order to establish certain continuities and discontinuities between the uses of fantasy here and in the later imaginative writings. In *The Pilgrim's Regress,* then, fantasy seems to function religiously as a means for leading the nonbeliever *toward* belief. It breaks down his "modern" prejudice against Christianity by exposing the emptiness of much of institutional religion, the flimsiness of certain antireligious intellectual or artistic fads, the inhumanity of some stern moralisms and ideologies, and the ultimate inadequacy of certain things which are good in themselves but only if subordinated to Christian faith. It also attempts—though with less effectiveness—to suggest the quality of Christian experience, both of what is lived here and now and what is hoped for ultimately.

The Screwtape Letters and *The Great Divorce,* both written after Lewis had begun the new, more "modern" venture in fantasy represented by *Out of the Silent Planet,* resemble Lewis' earlier work in their reliance on traditional forms and devices—epistolary satire in one book and in the other, the dream-vision. They retain little or nothing, however, of the autobiographical substructure of *The Pilgrim's Regress;* the story here is the supernatural struggle over the soul of man rather than the journey of spiritual quest.

In *The Screwtape Letters*[6] the object of that struggle is a young Englishman (circa World War II) who is trying to find his way to Christian faith and then to move forward in the Christian life. Fantasy enters the story only as a means for objectifying the forces contending for his soul. The agent of the Evil One is a relatively inexperienced tempter named Wormwood, and he is assisted through letters written from Hell by his superior (who is also his uncle),

Screwtape. It is a "devil's-eye view" which we are given. Traditional Christian values are set forth by an apparently uncomprehending opponent. The other edge of the ironic blade is also applied; attitudes which the worldly reader would presumably take for granted as normal, enlightened, or up to date are spoken of by Screwtape as part of the devilishly subtle scheme for inhibiting faith. Comic verbal effects further emphasize this ironic reversal of values; the devils speak of "Our Father Below," the "Lowerarchy," and even "the Miserific Vision."

The value of fantasy in relation to belief is hinted at in one of Screwtape's admonishments to the junior tempter. "Think of your young man," Screwtape writes,

> as a series of concentric circles, his will being the innermost, his intellect coming next, and finally his fantasy. You . . . must keep on shoving all the virtues outward till they are finally located in the circle of fantasy, and all the desirable qualities inward toward the Will [p. 37].

Lewis' way, too, is to work on the fantasy, with the hope of influencing the intellect and thus eventually moving the will.

One further question should be asked concerning the place of fantasy in this book: Is the fantasy meant to point only to subjective moral reality, or is it also intended to image objective supernatural reality? In the preface to the 1961 edition Lewis makes it clear that he believes in the existence of devils—not, he says, as "part of my creed but in the sense that it is one of my opinions."[7] But he asserts that it is not necessary for the reader to hold this opinion also.

> To those who share that opinion, my devils will be symbols of a concrete reality: to others, they will be personifications of abstractions, and the book will be an allegory. But it makes little difference which way you read it. For of course its purpose was not to speculate about diabolical life but to throw light from a new angle on the life of men.[8]

"Mansoul" is also being besieged in *The Great Divorce*.[9] Here, however, it is not evil which is trying to subvert faith, but Heaven which is trying to draw men away from Hell. Lewis makes use of the dream framework once again, because he wants to emphasize that this *is* a fantasy world, that "the trans-mortal conditions are solely an imaginative supposal: they are not even a guess or a speculation at what may actually await us" (p. viii). In his dream, Lewis (or the "I" of the narrative) goes with several of the dead by celestial omnibus to the outlying regions of Heaven, a place from which one must either go on, toward the Mountains, or back, to Hell. There he encounters the "bright" or "solid" people. In their presence he thinks for a moment that his fellow passengers have turned to transparent ghosts, "man-shaped stains on the brightness of that air." Then he realizes that the men are as they always were. "It was the light, the grass, the trees that were different," our narrator tells us; "made of some different substance, so much solider than things in our country that men were ghosts by comparison" (p. 19).

Explanations of these things are provided—as they are in that greatest of all fantasies about the state of souls after death—by a guide. Lewis' guide in Heaven is the nineteenth-century Scottish novelist, fantasist, and religious thinker George Macdonald. His *Phantastes* was for Lewis "what the first sight of Beatrice had been to Dante: *Here begins the New Life*" (p. 61). All those who have come on the bus, Macdonald says, are being given the opportunity of choosing or rejecting Reality. If they accept, Grey Town which they have left will turn out to have been Purgatory; and the "Valley of the Shadow of Life" where they are now will have been, from the beginning of their stay, Heaven. If they reject Reality they must return to what will now be seen as Hell. "Good and evil, when they are full grown, become retrospective" (p. 63).

Those who say no to Heaven do so for a variety of reasons. Some will not submit—they demand their "rights"; some are cynical and take the promises to be mere propaganda; some try various sins, or substitutes for Reality, such as sensuality or the lust for fame; essentially they all choose self instead of the Other. Lewis sets forth these refusals by way of satiric fantasy. The narrator overhears some Ghosts telling the Celestials all about Hell, and even accusing them of leading a "sheltered life." He sees a Ghost whose only concern is to steal one of the solid, golden apples but who learns that he can barely lift it.

The other function of fantasy, in relation to the ideal (in the imagery of this book, the Real) is also important. What must above all be established is the fact that Heaven is other than a "state of mind." Subjectivism is dealt with in a lengthy debate between a liberal Episcopal Ghost and his "narrow" literalistic former colleague. The Bright Person bluntly calls the bishop's liberalism a denial of the faith. "When in our whole lives," he asks, "did we honestly face, in solitude, the one question on which all turned: whether after all the Supernatural might not in fact occur? When did we put up one moment's real resistance to the loss of our faith?" (pp. 33–34). But this is meaningless to the Episcopal Ghost. After further conversation, Lewis tells us, "the Ghost nodded its head and beamed on the Spirit with a bright clerical smile . . . and then turned away humming softly to itself 'City of God, how broad and far'" (p. 40).

But thought must also be given to the relation between Heaven and earth, between the eternal state and the choice made in time. Does this life simply "develop" into the life-to-come? No; as the title implies, there is no "marriage of Heaven and Hell," but a "great divorce." "There are only two kinds of people in the end: those who say to God, 'Thy will be done,' and those to whom God says, in the end, '*Thy* will be done'" (p. 69). Yet Eternity is solid and Time insubstantial. God is sovereign; how can man not be a mere puppet? We are compelled, Macdonald reminds the narrator, to put the question about Eternity from within Time ("Time is the very lens through which ye see"); we must simply make our choice of ways, in the experience of freedom, and not try to leap into Eternity to see the final state of all things. In other words, the question is referred to mystery—first by way of Macdonald's discourse (pp. 128–29) and then by way of an image:

> I saw a great assembly of gigantic forms all motionless, all in deepest silence, standing forever about a little silver table and looking upon it. And on the table there were little figures like chessmen who went to and fro doing this and that. And I knew that each chessman was the *idolum* or puppet representative of some one of the great presences that stood by. And the acts and motions of each chessman were a moving portrait, a mimicry or pantomime, which delineated the inmost nature of his giant master. And these chessmen are men

and women as they appear to themselves and to one another in this world. And the silver table is Time. And those who stand and watch are the immortal souls of those same men and women [p. 130].

What makes *The Great Divorce* different from the books already looked into is the considerable amount of "unassigned" imagery: imagery not required by, though consonant with, the allegory—and therefore tending to create a *mythic* dimension which suggests not just moral concepts but the "feel" of transcendent Reality. The most successful use of fantasy is still in its negative, satirical function; but in this work fantasy moves more convincingly toward the sublime. Except for a few overwritten pages near the end about the apotheosis of "Sarah Smith of Golders Green," Lewis relies on the consistency of his images rather than on the incantatory rhythm of his syntax.

Out of the Silent Planet[10] sets aside the traditional frameworks for allegory in favor of the modern vehicle known as science fiction. "The idea of other planets," writes C. S. Lewis in 1955, looking back upon earlier years,

exercised upon me then a peculiar, heady attraction, which was quite different from any other of my literary interests. . . . The interest, when the fit was upon me, was ravenous, like a lust. . . . I may perhaps add that my own planetary romances have been not so much the gratification of that fierce curiosity as its exorcism. The exorcism worked by reconciling it with, or subjecting it to, the other, the more elusive, and genuinely imaginative, impulse.[11]

What he looks for in science fiction, then, is never merely scientific "gimmicks," nor novel ways of presenting "well-worn Tellurian stories of / Crooks, spies, conspirators, or love," but something beyond all this, something related to a "genuinely imaginative impulse." As he asks in a poem of 1959:

> Why should I leave this green-floored cell,
> Roofed with blue air, in which we dwell,
> Unless, outside its guarded gates,
> Long, long desired, the Unearthly waits,
> Strangeness that moves us more than fear,
> Beauty that stabs with tingling spear,
> Or Wonder, laying on one's heart

That finger-tip at which we start
As if some thought too swift and shy
For reason's grasp had just gone by?[12]

Elwin Ransom, a Cambridge philologist on a walking tour, is kidnapped and taken to Malacandra (Mars) by a man named Devine and his scientist-associate, Professor Weston. The technical explanation of the space journey ("You may say we work by exploiting the less observed properties of solar radiation") is less detailed, though perhaps no more implausible, than that which Lewis found in one of his models, H. G. Wells's *The First Men in the Moon*. From Wells, too, no doubt, come Ransom's horrified imaginings as to what the extraterrestrial beings will be like: "bulbous eyes, grinning jaws, horns, stings, mandibles . . ." (p. 33).

But Lewis borrows from Wells at this point only in order to repudiate these images. Once again Lewis is using fantasy in order to clear away misconceptions about what may be "out there"—not out there in space so much as in that transcendental mode of being for which his space is merely an analogue. Space itself Ransom finds to be not the nightmarish "black, cold vacuity" "long engendered in the modern mind by the mythology that follows in the wake of science," but an empyrean ocean of radiance which he feels constrained to rechristen "the heavens" (pp. 29–30).

After the landing Ransom escapes from Weston and Devine. The Malacandrians he meets turn out to be of three different species, all with rationality, speech, and culture: the gentle, animal-seeming *hrossa;* the thin, elongated, intellectual bipeds called *sorns;* and the little froglike craftsmen, the *pfifltriggi*. Ransom is first befriended and taught by the *hrossa*. Their lore provides material for satirical references to such unnatural conditions on earth as war, incontinence and adultery, social injustice, and atheism. More of the same comes by way of the *sorns*. Like the king of Brobdingnag, they express astonishment at what is told them of human history—of war, slavery, and prostitution. When Ransom is permitted to look at his world (which they call Thulcandra, the "silent planet") through their equivalent of a telescope, it is "the bleakest moment in all his travels" (p. 103).

The mythic possibilities of fantasy are also put to use. Malacandra is ruled by the Oyarsa, aided by innumerable *eldils*. *Eldils* are something like Aquinas' notion of angels ("the body of an *eldil* is a movement swift as light"). Over all of them, creator and ruler of the whole universe in fact, is Maleldil the Young, a spiritual being who "lives with the Old One." At Meldilorn, where he has been taken by one of the *sorns,* Ransom meets the Oyarsa and learns more. Thulcandra has been a silent planet, he is told, since it was spoiled by the Bent Oyarsa ("bent" is their metaphor for evil), but it has been besieged by Maleldil. The prophecies are that the siege of Thulcandra may be near its end.

Weston or the forces behind Weston are the enemy, during these days near the end; and "the dangers to be feared are not planetary but cosmic, or at least solar, and they are not temporal but eternal" (p. 167). Weston represents the kind of fusion of life-force philosophy and technological imperialism which for Lewis was the worst manifestation of scientism. In the myth Weston stands for the modern *hubris* which, not being satisfied with what humanity has done to its own world, now wishes to make the interplanetary leap. Lewis' most devastating satire comes when Weston stands before the Oyarsa, explaining the life-force ideology by which he justifies his galactic imperialism. Ransom, having learned the language, interprets for him, and what sounds fairly impressive in Weston's euphemistic jargon becomes brutal and ruthless in Malacandrian terms. At one point, in fact, Ransom is made to protest: "I cannot say what he says, Oyarsa, in your language" (pp. 146–49).

Although the names used are Maleldil and Oyarsa, C. S. Lewis is clearly presenting a cosmology and an understanding of God and man analogous to those of traditional Christian belief. Maleldil, Ransom realizes, is "a spirit without body, parts, or passions" (p. 70).[13] The *eldils* are angels, the Oyarsa an archangel. The Oyarsa tells Ransom that, although they are in many ways unlike, they are both "copies of Maleldil." Bent as the term for evil suggests Augustine's (and Luther's) use of the word *curvatus* with reference to the sin that moves a man to turn from God, concupiscently, toward the world or toward himself. The entire "silent planet" myth, of course, is based on mythical, apocalyptic hints from the Bible.

But the descriptions of Malacandrian geography and culture are freighted also with archetypal images not clearly analogous to any part of the Christian story. Similarly, the "eloquence" that characterizes a number of passages in the book tends to evoke not a specifically Christian response to the supernatural but a generalized sense of the numinous.

> Like a silence spreading over a room full of people, like an infinitesimal coolness on a sultry day, like a passing memory of some long-forgotten sound or scent, like all that is stillest and smallest and most hard to seize in nature, Oyarsa passed between his subjects and drew near and came to rest, not ten yards away from Ransom in the center of Meldilorn. Ransom felt a tingling of his blood and a pricking on his fingers as if lightning were near him; and his heart and body seemed to him to be made of water [pp. 128–29].

Out of the Silent Planet departs in several respects from Lewis' practice in the more strictly allegorical works. One notices first of all the "popular" form, that of the space voyage, which makes possible once again the twofold reference, through satire and myth, to this world and the other. It is to emphasize the otherworldly reference that Lewis eliminates the dream framework and turns to science fiction. Here we have myth handled as "fact" and the natural metaphors within the myths as cosmic "facts." Within the story itself Ransom is made to state Lewis' own understanding of "pagan" myth in relation to reality: "It had dawned on him that the recurrent human tradition of bright, elusive people might after all have another explanation than the anthropologists had yet given" (pp. 101–2); it had even occurred to him "that the distinction between history and mythology might be itself meaningless outside the Earth" (p. 157).

It is clear also that *Out of the Silent Planet,* as fictional apologetic, is meant to be only implicitly (rather than explicitly) Christian. In chapter 22 and the postscript the narrator steps forward to announce that "it is time to remove the mask and acquaint the reader with the real and practical purpose for which this book has been written." He goes on to say that it was Ransom who first suggested, after his return to "Thulcandra," that they "publish in the form of *fiction* what would certainly not be listened to as fact." The account is to be set forth not as "total-explanation myth" but more as a *praeparatio evangelica*. In Ransom's words:

> What we need for the moment is not so much a body of belief as a body of people familiarized with certain ideas. If we could even effect in one per cent of our readers a change-over from the conception of Space to the conception of Heaven, we should have made a beginning [p. 167].

In *Perelandra*[14] C. S. Lewis moves further in the direction of myth-making. The science fiction device is handled even more cavalierly than in the earlier story. Ransom has been commissioned to go to Perelandra (Venus) and help repel some sort of attack by the Bent Oyarsa. But there is no spaceship; he is placed inside a kind of casket and whisked away, with no technological problem at all. After all, Ransom says, "a creature [the Oyarsa] who has kept a planet in its orbit for several billions of years will be able to manage a packing-case!" (p. 21). Because *Perelandra* is to such a great extent a sequel to and a further explanation of the "silent planet" myth, Lewis is obliged to provide a good deal of exposition. In chapter 1 (where the Malacandrian voyage is summarized and *eldils* explained) and in chapter 6 (where we are brought up to date on Professor Weston), a certain clumsiness and a clutter of detail lessen the story's impact.

Perelandra is the story of a second Eve in another Paradise. In fact, as Victor Hamm has suggested,[15] this is the story of Paradise Retained. Milton's *Paradise Lost* is indeed the closest analogue, and Lewis' own *Preface to Paradise Lost* provides the best commentary. *Out of the Silent Planet* can now be seen as a mythical exposition of the created order and the possibility of its perversion by evil (Genesis, chapters 1 and 2, or *Paradise Lost,* books 1 through 8). *Perelandra* gives the account of the temptation. This story of a fall that almost takes place is made the occasion for a critique of the *felix culpa* notion and a celebration of the unspeakable greatness of the redemption which came to our fallen world. The Christian significance of the story is rendered explicitly, not only in the archetypal action but also in a series of allusions. Facing Professor Weston, who has made himself the instrument of evil, Ransom is made to say: "I'm a Christian." Maleldil is specifically spoken of as having become incarnate on Earth. Much of the didactic content is incorporated in two long theological disputations between Ransom, speaking for theism, and Weston, with his pantheistic, emergent-evolution, life-spirit ideology.

The account of the temptation follows in a number of respects Milton's version of the Genesis story and incorporates some of the Augustinian notions about man which (according to the *Preface to Paradise Lost*) underlie it. (Adam—the King on Perelandra—is left out of Lewis' version, however, possibly because Lewis does not want to deal with the topic which he thinks Milton would have been better off avoiding: unfallen sexuality).[16] The Lady is unfallen, Edenic mankind. She is both goddess and madonna, so that in her presence Ransom feels a sense of shame over his somewhat ugly body. She knows no evil and lives in fellowship with the beasts and in direct communion with, and perfect obedience to, Maleldil, from whom she receives from time to time such knowledge as is needful. Through Ransom she becomes aware for the first time of her freedom ("I thought," she says, "that I was carried in the will of Him I love, but now I see that I walk with it" [p. 68]), and she informs him of the one prohibition. She lives on the islands, the floating lands which undulate with the waves; she is not to dwell on the Fixed Land. The image operates, in an almost Spenserian manner, to suggest the contrast between living by faith and seeking a rigid kind of security.

Weston initiates the ordeal by encouraging her to *think* about the Fixed Land, thus emphasizing the contrast between what is and what might be. He does what Screwtape recommended to Wormwood—he works upon fantasy, or imagination, first. Next comes the appeal to her desire for wisdom (which she calls "growing older"). Finally Weston urges her to exercise a kind of tragic courage. The commandment, he tells her, is a test, one which she can meet only by disobeying, by daring to be other than what she was created. (Ransom sees on her face at this point the look of a "tragedy queen.") Her capacity for self-consciousness, good in itself, is being made an avenue for temptation, so that it will produce bad self-awareness, egotism, and idolatry. The Fall, as Lewis reminds us in *Preface to Paradise Lost,* consisted simply in disobedience, and it resulted simply from pride.[17]

Thus far I have emphasized the traditional Christian elements in *Perelandra.* But Lewis makes important contributions of his own to this retelling of the ancient story. He, like Milton, universalizes the paradisaic experience by importing mythical materials from other traditions and archetypal patterns from the interior history of humanity. We are told that when Ransom woke to his first morning in Perelandra

> he saw reality, and thought it was a dream. He opened his eyes and saw a strange heraldically colored tree loaded with yellow fruits and silver leaves. Round the base of the indigo stem was coiled a small dragon covered with scales of red gold. He recognized the garden of the Hesperides at once [p. 41].

The Lady, when he meets her, seems to him to be not only Eve and the Madonna but also Artemis. The landscape of Venus has something of the same effect on us as the Paradise of Milton's poem, and Ransom has "a sensation not of following an adventure but of enacting a myth" (p. 44). Again we are asked to ponder the relationship of myth to reality. "Were all the things which appeared as mythology on earth scattered through other worlds as realities?" (p. 41).

> Long since on Mars, and more strongly since he came to Perelandra, Ransom had been perceiving that the triple distinction of truth from myth and of both from fact was purely terrestrial—was part and parcel of that unhappy division between soul and body which resulted from the Fall. Even on earth the sacraments existed as a permanent reminder that the division was neither wholesome nor final. The Incarnation had been the beginning of its disappearance [p. 149].

Lewis also imposes on the mythic base his own notion of how temptation rationalizes itself for modern man. Weston represents scientism, a specifically modern manifestation of pride and a contemporary venture in the direction of the false infinite and self-deification. But Weston becomes an archetypal figure, a being possessed by something which is both superhuman and subhuman.

His voice and manner change from time to time, so that occasionally he is for a moment merely the Weston that Ransom remembers, whimpering helplessly about "them" and what "they" are doing to him. But, most often, he is represented as a "motiveless malignity" called the Un-man. This embodiment of evil is dealt with in a way suited to mythic narrative; Ransom does not outargue him, he literally and physically fights him. As "ransom" he risks his life to save the Lady's innocence. Appropriately, then, as the fight begins the Un-man cries aloud, in hideous parody, the words once heard on Golgotha—"*Eloi, Eloi, lama sabachthani?*" (pp. 159–60).

The fact that Ransom wins this fight points to the most significant thematic modification Lewis has attempted. He has taken his stand against the *felix culpa*. Countering Weston's use of the *felix peccatum Adae* argument, Ransom tells the Lady: "The first King and first Mother of our world did the forbidden thing; and He brought good out of it in the end. But what they did was not good; and what they lost we have not seen" (p. 125). It is the image of what they lost that Lewis now gives us to see. Before finally defeating the Un-man, Ransom is plunged with him down into the depths of the sea and then sent upward again into a subterranean cave.

After bashing the Un-man's face in with a stone, Ransom (now with a wound in his heel) has to make his way from this under-ground world, first upward and then outward, to a clear pool on a high mountaintop. There, after many days of healing rest and pleasure, in a setting whose unimaginable beauty can only be hinted at, he meets with the Oyeresu of Malacandra and Perelandra, who take form in his presence as the giant figures of Mars and Venus. There also he sees the Lady and her King, archetypal man and woman, identified—for mythological resonance—by the names "Oyarsa-Perelendri, the Adam, the Crown, Tor and Tinidril, Baru and Baru'ah, Ask and Embla, Yatsur and Yatsurah" (p. 220). He learns that they have been elevated by Maleldil to full power and rule over their planet. (In the *Preface to Paradise Lost* Lewis reminds us of Milton's—and Augustine's—theory that if there had been no Fall, the human race would have been promoted to angelic status.[18])

Finally, before his return to Earth, Ransom is given a prophecy of the end of earthly history and a vision of the eternal Reality, which Lewis presents—first in paradoxical and hieratic words spoken by the *eldils* and then in a riot of visual imagery—as the Great Dance, in which "all the secular generalities of which history tells," the individual entities of nature, all personal beings, and even universal truths or qualities are revealed as "a whole solid figure" of "enamoured and inter-inanimated circlings," and that figure in turn as the "mere superficies of a far vaster pattern in four dimensions" (pp. 234-35).

As in the first book of the trilogy, we readers are ushered into these fantastic scenes and events by someone with hindering doubts and preconceptions. This time it is not Ransom—for he has been convinced—but the narrator of the launch and reentry, identified in chapter 2 as "Lewis." The fact that the author "frames" Ransom's story by means of "Lewis'" common-sense skepticism and fear of being "drawn in" suggests that we are once again the targets of a literary-apologetic "strategy." We may be "drawn into" an allegorical reading—in which case the personages and incidents of the Perelandrian expedition speak to us of our moral being. ("To construct plausible and moving 'other worlds,'" Lewis once wrote, "you must draw on the only real 'other world' we know, that of the spirit."[19]) They speak to us of what we are *in potentia,* as created in the image of God; of how temptation comes and how real the moral struggle is; and of the higher levels of self-integration and insight which moral victory can bring. They also speak, in satirical tones, of the special intellectual shapes of self-deception which evil has taken in our day.

But it is clear that this is not enough. Half of Lewis' very brief preface consists in the warning that "all the human characters in this book are purely fictitious and none of them is allegorical"—which means that we are to be "drawn into" a symbolical-mythic reading. It is for this reason that so much richness of imagery and allusion and so much eloquence in prose rhythms have been imparted to the texture of this work. At certain points Lewis' prose is apparently meant to achieve, within its limitations, something like the grandeur or elevation of the Miltonic music.

Nothing else in C. S. Lewis (except, perhaps, *Till We Have Faces*) so clearly intends the mythopoeic. To a considerable extent it succeeds. Many readers of this book have had, like Ransom, the sensation of "enacting a myth." Part of the pleasure arises out of the dialectic in which the knowing reader finds himself involved, between the experience of Paradise Lost and the ideal, hypothetical possibility of Paradise Retained. For some the power lies in Lewis' ability to make real the manifestations of great supernatural beings. Most readers, however, remember longest the colors and scents, the floating islands, the mythological creatures. Perhaps a few even begin to suspect that some reality objectively exists, the experience of which would "feel something like" the imaginative experience that comes by way of Lewis' mythopoeic power.

What is hoped, of course, is that the reader will grasp the similarity between the quality of the Perelandrian scenes and happenings and the quality of Reality as understood by orthodox Christianity, in terms of God, Providence, angels and devils, the Incarnation, and the unity of all things in God's creative act. Lewis takes too many measures, however, to see to it that the reader cannot fail to entertain this possibility. (It is simply too much to have Ransom, about to hurl the stone into the Un-man's face, say: "In the name of the Father and of the Son and of the Holy Ghost, here goes—I mean Amen" [p. 193].) On this point many are likely to share the opinion of Marjorie Nicolson (who very much liked *Out of the Silent Planet*) that even though "the second world of Venus is descriptively more beautiful than the earlier world of Mars, . . . in *Perelandra* the Christian apologist has temporarily eclipsed the poet and artist."[20]

The concluding work in the trilogy, *That Hideous Strength*,[21] seems to have been influenced by the fictional techniques of Charles Williams. Instead of being taken from this world to another one, we become involved with alien forces which irrupt into our world. Because of the humdrum scenes and persons of the opening chapters (Lewis claims, in his preface, to be following the pattern of the traditional fairy tale), the unsophisticated reader making his way unwarily through the book will probably be more than one third of the way through before he begins to realize in what an outrageous dance he is being led. There are, of course, the dreams, which seem to have some connection with actual people and happenings; and there is some serious talk about magic. It is Jane Studdock who has the puzzling dreams. Jane is the wife of Mark Studdock, a fellow of Bracton College, in Edgestow. The talk of magic comes from the Dimbles, an older couple in the university with whom Jane is acquainted.

But everything else seems down to earth enough. After only six months the marriage is already in some trouble; this seems to be one strand of the plot. Through a certain Lord Feverstone (who turns out to be the Dick Devine of the voyage to Malacandra), Mark receives an opportunity to take a leave from Bracton and join the staff of a scientific institute at nearby Belbury, the National Institute of Coordinated Experiments; Mark's relations with the N.I.C.E. people seems to be another strand. Jane, frightened by her dreams, is advised by the Dimbles to see a Miss Ironwood at a place called St. Anne's-on-the-Hill; Jane's involvement with the group at St. Anne's is the third strand.

After prolonged uncertainty about the precise nature of his responsibilities at Belbury, Mark (who is a sociologist) finally settles for writing newspaper propaganda. He commits himself in this way despite some qualms about N.I.C.E. tactics. Meanwhile, Jane has learned that there is a "company" at St. Anne's led by a mysterious Mr. Fisher-King and that they want her to join them. Unable to believe that her dreams are veridical and unwilling to commit herself, Jane hesitates. She makes her decision, finally, after seeing in the flesh the sinister figure who has appeared in her dreams.

It is at this point that the rope which has secured our fictional balloon to actuality is irrevocably cut. Jane now meets Mr. Fisher-King. She learns that he was originally a philologist named Elwin Ransom, that he has been on other planets and has held converse with their tutelary spirits, and that he is on earth now to combat a conspiracy against mankind. Jane is important to the Company because she has "true" dreams which foretell the actions of the enemy, whose initials, of course, are N.I.C.E.

Mark, meanwhile, has been let in on what is really happening at Belbury. The goals of N.I.C.E. are vast and utopian—and totalitarian. Its "Head" is literally that—the severed head of Alcasan, an Arab radiologist executed for murder, kept "alive" by an ingenious mechanism. Mark's superiors now reveal that they want Jane, because of her "gift." Unable to take her by force they put pressure on Mark to lure her to Belbury. When he fails to do so, they have him arrested and imprison him in one of their own cells to undergo "brainwashing."

But just as the higher good Powers are fighting on the side of the St. Anne's group and the evil powers (called "macrobes") are behind N.I.C.E. and its "Head," so there is also one possibly "neutral" power that each side wants to enlist. Under Bragdon Wood (the heart of ancient Logres, the "true" Britain of King Arthur's time) lies buried the great magician of Logres: Merlin. After fifteen hundred years or so of "sleep," he is coming to life. Because of Jane's dreams and the leadership of Ransom (now revealed as Pendragon of ancient Logres), Merlin sides with the St. Anne's "remnant."

After receiving into himself the powers of the planetary spirits— Mercury, Venus, Mars, Saturn, and Jupiter—Merlin goes to Belbury, supposedly as the interpreter for the false "Merlin" they have found. During an after-dinner speech by the director of N.I.C.E., Merlin works his magic. First he turns the words of all the Belbury people into nonsense ("They that have despised the word of God," he cries in Latin, "from them shall the word of man also be taken away"), then looses upon them the animals they have kept caged for purposes of vivisection. After he helps Mark to escape, Mark sets out for St. Anne's-on-the-Hill. All the N.I.C.E. leaders are killed, Belbury burns, and Edgestow is destroyed by an earthquake and floods.

At St. Anne's, Ransom gives his farewell blessing to the members of the Company. The forces of evil having been, for a time, thwarted, he is returning to Venus. Mark and Jane are about to be reunited. Because of the change of heart he has undergone at Belbury and because of what the Director and the others at St. Anne's have taught her, the reader feels an assurance, at the end, that the marriage, too, has been set right.

The influence of Charles Williams may be discerned in more than just the "novelistic" handling of setting and character. It is also reflected in the Arthurian materials which Lewis integrates with his own "silent planet" myth by way of the dichotomy of Britain and Logres and the figure of Merlin. It may also have something to do with the use in this book of the man-woman relationship (not prominent in the rest of Lewis' fiction) for both its dramatic and symbolic values. But just as Lewis makes something uniquely his own out of Logres and Merlin, so he characteristically underplays romantic love, which Williams would have made much of, and stresses instead—satirically—those factors in modern education and culture which are helping to drive Mark and Jane apart. The narrator of the story comments, for example, about Mark:

> It must be remembered that in Mark's mind hardly one rag of noble thought, either Christian or Pagan, had a secure lodging. His education had been neither scientific nor classical—merely "Modern." The severities both of abstraction and of high human tradition had passed him by: and he had neither peasant shrewdness nor aristocratic honor to help him. He was a man of straw, a glib examinee in subjects that require no exact knowledge . . . and the first hint of a real threat to his bodily life knocked him sprawling [p. 212].

But the Studdocks are more than just bad examples for us. More positively, they also exemplify our continuing bond with actuality, as the fantasy begins to carry us out of this world. And they serve as our guides in the good and evil worlds of St. Anne's and Belbury. Ransom is no longer our link, having become—as Pendragon and "Mr. Fisher-King"—a semimythical figure. For the most part Lewis filters the story alternately through Jane's consciousness and Mark's. We are to identify with their skepticism and their increasing openness toward belief.

The contrast between the two headquarters, Belbury and St. Anne's, is established with a certain artistic finesse. One encounters a garden, for instance, at both places. The one at St. Anne's, in its naturalness, reminds Jane of the garden in *Peter Rabbit*. The "Ornamental Pleasure Grounds" laid out by the Edwardian millionaire who built Belbury has an effect, we are told, like the appearance of a

municipal cemetery. At St. Anne's animals are free, tame, and play-
ful; at the other place they are kept in cages for vivisection.

The names of the N.I.C.E. people reveal Lewis' satirical intent.
Names like Wither, Frost, and Feverstone suggest blight and perversion. The good people have homely English-sounding names such
as Dimble, Maggs, and Denniston. When we meet Miss ("Fairy")
Hardcastle, the thickly built, short-haired, cigar-chewing virago who
heads the N.I.C.E. police, we recall that this is indeed a "fairy tale
for grown-ups."

Other differences become apparent through the life of each community. St. Anne's is all openness, courtesy, good conversation,
healthy domesticity, and relationships characterized by both hierarchy and equality. Belbury is secrecy, vagueness, uncertainty about
one's status, perversion of the normal ("Fairy" Hardcastle and the
treble-voiced Filostrato are illustrations of what this evil world does
to sexuality), an artificial life of neither laughter nor tears.

What is being planned at Belbury is likewise a perversion of the
natural. The planners wish to study and manipulate men. But in
the words of William Hingest, Mark's "reactionary" colleague from
Bracton, "You can't study men; you can only get to know them,
which is quite a different thing" (p. 73). N.I.C.E., we are told early
in the story, represents that constructive fusion between state and
laboratory on which so many thoughtful people base their hopes of a
better world. It actually represents, of course, precisely the kind of
scientism which Lewis abominated. The intentions of these men are
to "re-condition" all human beings, free the brain as much as possible
from all that is organic (the body, birth, breeding, and death), and
take control of the destiny of mankind. Such an enterprise is anti-
human, in Lewis' opinion, and will indeed bring about the "abolition
of man." Therefore Belbury must be brought down in ashes, through
the magic powers of Merlin.

As the story of Mark and Jane Studdock, *That Hideous Strength*
is a story of sin, repentance, and regeneration. Sin, understood as
pride, is bringing about an ever more virulent infection by modern
evil. The inoculation of evil that Mark receives renders him immune
to the worst of it, and he comes at least as far as repentance. The

B

healthful environment and medicinal grace of St. Anne's bring Jane even further.

But it is also a national battle, between legendary Logres and "mere Britain," which is "haunted" by Logres. Britain is secularism and rapidly extending chaos; Logres is loyalty to the divine will and to created Nature. Through Ransom's talk with Merlin we learn that the struggle is cosmic as well. Ransom tells him that no help can be expected from the British government, nor from the church, nor from "Christian princes," or from the emperor, nor from the heathen "beyond Byzantium."

> "However far you went, you would find the machines, the crowded cities, the empty thrones, the false writings, the barren beds: men maddened with false promises and soured with true miseries, worshipping the iron works of their own hands, cut off from Earth their mother and from the Father in Heaven. . . . The Hideous Strength holds all this Earth in its fist to squeeze as it wishes" [p. 346].

Mythically we have moved from the unfallen creation of Malacandra through the temptation in the Eden of Perelandra to the arrogance of idolatrous civilization and the judgment of Babel.

It is to be seen, finally, then, as a battle of Heaven and Hell, of *eldils* and "macrobes," of Maleldil and the Bent Eldil. The blockade of the "silent planet" has been broken, and the Powers of Deep Heaven come down to empower Merlin, to save the world, Logres, and St. Anne's, and to bring Mark and Jane together again. As in *Perelandra,* therefore, biblical and other traditional Christian allusions surround the supposedly neutral mythic material. The equivalences of the "silent planet" myth hold here as well, and the powers behind N.I.C.E. are clearly demonic agencies representing Hell.

That Hideous Strength is less successful than either of the other books in the trilogy. It attempts too much. Here, more than anywhere else in Lewis' fiction, we are led to expect three-dimensional characterization, of the Studdocks at least. But the distance between the narrator and Mark makes it almost impossible for us to feel with Mark or even to care much about what happens to him. If we concentrate on the moral satire, we can overlook to some extent the failure in characterization. And it is true that the impression one receives from the first half of the book is predominantly that of the skillful satirical dissection of Mark and Jane, Bracton College, and N.I.C.E. But as mythical elements emerge at the St. Anne's pole they are matched in the Belbury narrative by elements of the grotesque: the severed but breathing "Head," the "macrobes," the surrealistic pictures and unsymmetrical chambers by which Mark is being re-conditioned, the weird ritual killings of Straik and Filostrato.

But in any case Lewis is depending not so much on satire and its allegorical bent as on mythopoeic power. The whole first section of chapter 15, for example, is a set piece on the "descent of the gods," the empowering of Merlin by the planetary Oyeresu. In this story, however, the satiric and grotesque elements tend to overwhelm the mythic ones. The myth itself seems synthetic and contrived. Lewis has been left with mythical apparatus from the earlier books which has to be made relevant to the new earthly setting and has to be integrated with the Arthurian material he now wishes to introduce. The welding does not hold, the machinery creaks and groans, and the result has neither the haunting simplicity nor the focused intensity required for mythopoeic power.

Fantasy that fails to rise into myth falls back toward allegory. But then everything depends on maintaining the creative tension between the idea which controls the work and the story framework which is its vehicle. In several respects, however, the tension is weakened. This failure is noticeable, here and there, because of obtrusive comment from the author. When Professor Frost is about to die in the fire set by his own hand, for instance, we hear the voice of the narrator, sermonizing:

> Not till then did his controllers allow him to suspect that death itself might not after all cure the illusion of being a soul—nay, might prove the entry into a world where that illusion raged infinite and unchecked. Escape for the soul, if not for the body, was offered him. He became able to know (and simultaneously refused the knowledge) that he had been wrong from the beginning, that souls and personal responsibility existed [p. 247].

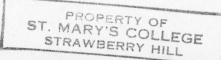

Even more importantly, the tension collapses with regard to the change that takes place in the Studdocks. Lewis dramatizes the new possibilities by confronting Mark with the emblematic figure of a woman "divinely tall, part naked, part wrapped in a flame-colored robe" and by surrounding Jane with "liquid light and supernatural warmth" (p. 458). As Wayne Shumaker remarks: "Disembodied spirit is permitted to take matters out of the hands of human agents." And this failure is serious, "for it is not on Mars or Venus, but on Earth, that the real test of the Christian world-view must come."[22]

But if the tension between the fiction and the idea collapses, then a heavier burden falls on belief. Unless the reader can implicitly accept the fiction's commitment to the values of the *hypothetical* world which the writer has constructed, he will begin to examine Lewis' ideas in their own right. If he finds them unbelievable, he will find the novel unbearable. Lewis' failure, in that case, will be the more ironic, for it is precisely the modern unbeliever whom the strategy of fantasy and myth is supposed to disarm.

Although religious ideas and beliefs are obviously at the center of the literary fantasy written by C. S. Lewis, I have until now confined myself to sequential and structural questions. What sorts of experience is the reader likely to undergo as he makes his way from the beginning to the end of a particular book, and from the beginning of *The Pilgrim's Regress* through the end of *That Hideous Strength*? How do style, tone, characterization, "plot," and narrative technique correlate with this unique sequence of interests, concerns, and excitements? The religious themes and apologetic intent of this fiction raise other kinds of questions as well. I must at this point, therefore, "place" the literary structure within the cosmos of Lewis' theological thought—the pattern of beliefs implied by the images of his space myth and rendered explicitly in such nonfictional apologetics as *The Case for Christianity, Miracles, The Problem of Pain,* and other books and papers.

C. S. Lewis speaks often of his adherence to "plain, central Christianity" or "mere Christianity." Within this traditional structure of doctrine, however, he concerns himself chiefly not so much with questions concerning Redemption (Atonement, Salvation, Sanctification) as with the relationship of God as Creator to his creation. This is consistent, of course, with his often stated special interest in the *praeparatio evangelica* as distinct from *evangelium* itself. But when we ask what Lewis conceives to be the actual qualities of the relation between Creator and creature, we discover an imbalance. In every confrontation between man and the Eternal Word who mediates the love and power of God's being, between man and the supernatural instruments of God's will, or between man and the natural reflectors of God's self-disclosure, there is an excessive sense of "otherness." Lewis tends, in short, very greatly to emphasize transcendence over immanence, eternity over time, objectivity over subjectivity, and the supernatural over the natural. Even if, as some would maintain, this is a tendency inherent in traditional Christian theism itself, we would have to see in Lewis something of a "skewed" orthodoxy.

It is a kind of transcendence which is impressed upon Ransom in his dealings with the *eldils,* an "otherness" which brings a sense of the numinous. The Oyarsa tells him: "I am not 'here' altogether as you are, Ransom of Thulcandra. Creatures of your kind must drop out of heaven into a world; for us the worlds are places in heaven" (*Out of the Silent Planet,* p. 130). God and creatures, the analogy implies, are incommensurable. "The very words 'to be,'" writes Lewis in more abstract terms, "cannot be applied to Him and to them in exactly the same sense."[23]

Lewis also ascribes to deity the more controversial property of "impassibility." In the myth it is hinted at in the description of the embodied Mars and Venus in *Perelandra:*

> One single, changeless expression . . . was stamped on each and there was nothing else there at all. . . . What this one thing was he could not be certain. He concluded in the end that it was charity. But it was terrifyingly different from the expression of human charity, which we always see either blossoming out of, or hastening to descend into, natural affection. Here there was no affection at all. . . . Pure, spiritual, intellectual love shot from the faces like barbed lightning [p. 213].

If God's nature excludes "affection," it even more obviously excludes the possibility for him of pain. As Lewis puts it, there is "something which God, in His own nature, never does at all—to surrender, to suffer, to submit, to die. Nothing in God's nature corresponds to this process at all."[24] Even some traditionalists, however, have wanted to insist, with Langmead Casserley, that "there can be a conception of pain in God which avoids the patripassian heresy," a pain which is "the expression and inevitable by-product of his love."[25]

God is also eternal; he transcends passage. But how, then, is his perfect and eternal knowing related to our allegedly free acts in time? As we have seen in *The Great Divorce*, Lewis tends to dissolve this question in the general mystery of the divine transcendence. Just as God's being is incommensurable with our mode of being, so his knowing infinitely transcends all that can be hinted at by our use of the verb know. God, in eternity, the *nunc stans*, can never be said, for example, to foresee but only to see.[26] As for time, history enters into Ransom's vision of the Great Dance only as

. minute corpuscles of momentary brightness . . . the secular generalities of which history tells—peoples, institutions, climates of opinion, civilizations, arts, sciences, and the like—ephemeral coruscations that piped their short song and vanished [*Perelandra*, p. 234].

Lewis is at pains to emphasize the traditional notion of the objectivity and substantiality of Being. God is Eternal Fact, the Episcopal Ghost is told, not the Supreme Value (*The Great Divorce*, p. 38). One of the epigrams included in Walter Hooper's edition of Lewis' poems is an emendation for the ending of Goethe's *Faust*. The way its imagery reverses Goethe's is startling confirmation of the tendency in question.

> Solids whose shadows lay
> Across time, here
> (All subterfuge dispelled)
> Show hard and clear;
> Fondled impossibles
> Wither outside;
> Within, the Wholly Masculine
> Confronts His bride.[27]

Man's *Sehnsucht*—his intense longing—and the myths in which he expresses it, point him toward something which has objective reality. Myths are not mere projections of human longing. They are "good dreams" sent by God, real though unfocused gleams of divine truth falling on the human imagination from the great, sovereign, un-created, unconditioned Reality at the core of things.[28]

There is, of course, a strong suggestion of Platonic as well as Christian transcendentalism in all this. People in Lewis' fantasies are always encountering archetypal forms which cause them to reflect adversely on the phantasmal copies which they have hitherto es-teemed as real. When Jane Studdock meets the semidivinized Ransom, she savors for the first time "the word *King* itself with all its linked associations of battle, marriage, priesthood, mercy, and power" (*That Hideous Strength,* p. 160). When Ransom tastes the water of Perelandra, it is "almost like meeting Pleasure itself for the first time" (*Perelandra,* p. 30). He is prostrated by the first sight of the glorified King and Queen and says brokenly: "I have never before seen a man or a woman. I have lived all my life among shadows and broken images" (*Perelandra,* p. 219).

It can also be shown, I think, that C. S. Lewis tends to derogate the natural excessively to enhance the supernatural. The natural man is presented, of course, as fallen, as a candidate for grace, incapable of grasping for himself the power that grace offers to his freedom. In this Lewis simply stands, with all the orthodox, against Pelagius and with Augustine. Like Augustine, too, as one of the "twice-born," Lewis stresses what Hügel called the "costingness" of regeneration. Thus, with *Prometheus Unbound* in mind, Lewis says of Shelley: "No poet has felt more keenly, or presented more weightily the necessity for a complete unmaking and remaking of man, to be endured at the dark bases of his being."[29]

But there may also be, in Lewis' thought, a denigration even of man *as man,* in his essence as *imago dei.* Sometimes it comes through language redolent of the Platonism already pointed out. The celestials in *The Great Divorce* are Solid People, whereas the terrestrials are phantoms: "One could attend to them or ignore them at will as you do with the dirt on a window pane" (p. 18). On Malacandra, one of Ransom's most privileged moments comes when he sees the faces of Weston and Devine as "masses of lumped and puckered flesh of variegated color fringed in some bristling, dark substance," and then suddenly realizes he has been looking at the human form "with almost Malacandrian eyes" (*Out of the Silent Planet,* p. 135).

The present life, says Lewis in a paper entitled "Transposition," is a diminution, a symbol, a substitute: "If flesh and blood cannot inherit the Kingdom, that is not because they are too solid, too gross, too distinct, too 'illustrious with being.' They are too flimsy, too transitory, too phantasmal."[30]

Accordingly, although Lewis can say with Irenaeus that to receive salvation is to be made truly *human,* his more typical statements envision something beyond the natural, a process of being "taken right *out* of Nature, turned into 'gods.'" "It is not," he says, "like teaching a horse to jump better and better but like turning a horse into a winged creature."[31]

Lewis' colleague and friend Austin Farrer, writing after Lewis' death, suggested that this tendency of his thought was an expression of a residual idealism which he never completely outgrew. "Lewis was raised," he points out,

> in the tradition of an idealist philosophy which hoped to establish the reality of the mental subject, independently of, or anyhow in priority to, that of the bodily world. Though he moved some way from such positions, he was still able to overlook the full involvement of the reasonable soul in a random and perishable system.

For similar reasons, Farrer adds, Lewis' discussion of evil and pain is somewhat vitiated by extreme moralism, a tendency to view man too narrowly as a moral will and his relation to God as a purely moral affair.[32] The biblical view, Reinhold Niebuhr has reminded us, is that "the finiteness, dependence, and the insufficiency of man's mortal life are facts which belong to God's plan of creation and must be accepted with reverence and humility." The created world is never to be seen as a corruption of an original divine unity and eternity.[33]

Lewis also pays scant attention to man's *historical* nature, and he takes a generally negative attitude toward change. In *That Hideous Strength,* for example, the contrast between Belbury and St. Anne's seems to put science, technology, and sociology all on the Devil's side, against the countryside, domesticity, "Englishness," and the classical and transcendental traditions. If the one pole is not presented as simply bad, it is at least presented as far more inclined toward evil than the other. Lewis' consistent rejection of "modernity" makes one wonder, indeed, if there is any place in his thinking for the christological belief

> that He who became Incarnate is the Logos who has been at work in the whole created world, in nature and in man, in art and in science, in culture and in progress, and all in such wise that contemporary trends of thought . . . are not enemies to be fought but friends who can provide new illuminations of the truth that is in Christ.[34]

Lewis' tendency to exalt transcendence, eternity, objectivity, and the supernatural at the expense of immanence, temporality, subjectivity, and the natural is seen, finally, not only in the symbols of his "space myth" and in the assertions of his discursive writings, but—and most tellingly, perhaps—in the images and analogies which he invents to make these propositions clear and vivid. In the BBC talks published as *Beyond Personality* he suggests the nature of man's relation to his Creator in terms such as the following: We are statues or pictures with the "shape" or likeness of God but without the kind of life God has. "This world is a great sculptor's shop. We are the statues and there is a rumor going around the shop that some of us are some day going to come to life." We are tin soldiers. Because "one tin soldier—*real* tin, just like the rest of us—has come fully and splendidly alive," God can begin to " 'inject' His kind of life and thought" into us, turning us tin soldiers into live men.[35]

The orthodox tradition conceives of this otherness as having been overcome in the incarnate Christ. In C. S. Lewis' Christology, however, the emphasis is almost exclusively on the deity of Christ, rather than on the humanity. Professor Pittenger goes too far, in my judgment, when he attempts to show Lewis guilty of the Apollinarian and Eutychian (Monophysite) heresies[36]; but one must suspect him, nonetheless, of a one-sided orthodoxy. For him there seems to be little or no reciprocity in the incarnation. It is the "taking of the Manhood into God." Jesus was "one man in whom the created life, derived from his mother, allowed itself to be completely and perfectly tuned into the begotten life. The natural human creature in Him was taken up fully into the divine Son."[37] All reflects the power of the Higher to come down, of the greater to include the less.[38]

Again, the more casual images are symptomatic. Lewis is careful to say that in the miracles performed by Jesus the incarnate God does suddenly and locally something God has done or will do in general; that he writes in small letters what God writes in large in nature.[39] But more characteristically he speaks of the incarnation as "the inconceivable, the uncreated, the thing from beyond nature, striking down into nature like lightning." The metaphor which illumines his "silent planet" myth is that of a universe at war. We are living in enemy-occupied territory. "Christianity is the story of how the rightful king has landed, you might say landed in disguise, and is calling us all to take part in a great campaign of sabotage."[40] One analogy—which, since it stands alone, I dare not overemphasize —is especially disturbing:

> The Eternal Being, who knows everything and who created the whole universe became not only a man but (before that) a baby, and before that a *foetus* inside a woman's body. If you want to get the hang of it, think of how you'd like to become a slug or a crab.[41]

What is the path by which this powerless creature, man, is brought into his destined relationship with the "Unimaginably and Insupportably Other" through this exalted God-man? Lewis rejects, of course, any suggestion that it is by way of man's search for God. (One might as well talk, he exclaims, about "the mouse's search for the cat"!) He has only scorn for the idea that one must align himself with the nisus toward value in the evolutionary process. As to the more narrowly historical situation, one finds it hard to imagine C. S. Lewis asking Bonhoeffer's question: "What is Jesus

Christ for us *today?*" No, grace is objective, it comes "from with-out"; and it is not so much tied to historical change as to the lasting things in our history and our nature—rationality, the sense of wonder, the beauties of nature, romantic love, poetry.

All this points to the work of grace called revelation. The event of revelation involves trust in or reliance upon God as made known to man in Jesus Christ (fiducia), arising out of an acquaintance (*notitia*) with the object of revelation and containing also an assent to certain affirmations that can be made about that object.[42] The issue for twentieth-century believers has concerned primarily the place given to belief, or assent. For Lewis, as for other modern theologians, faith as reliance is ultimately the most important thing. But in a typically "orthodox" way, he stresses the role of belief. He is not content, as many others are, to have it latent, and he wants to allow much less flexibility as to the extent to which it must become "patent." " 'Your belief' *means* 'what you think true.' And if you think one thing true, of course you must think the opposite false."[43] Belief is "assent to a proposition which we think so over-whelmingly probable that there is a psychological exclusion of doubt, though not a logical exclusion of dispute." When we assent, we find ourselves in a new situation, in the presence of God as Person. "What would, a moment before, have been variations in opinion, now become variations in your personal attitude to a Person."[44] Trust—in other words, fiducia; but belief remains prior.

C. S. Lewis as apologist, however, focuses on *notitia,* which for him signifies meaningful acquaintance with truthful propositions about the object of faith. In explicitly apologetic writings Lewis often assumes as a starting point a universal idea of a "Law of Nature or decent behavior." His fiction capitalizes on another means of enhancing the possibility of such acquaintance—the way of imagi-nation, the appeal to the sense of wonder. The "romantic experience" —of nature, love, or fantastic literature—can put a man on the way to God just as surely as can his search for truth or his awakened sense of right and wrong. This represents a "romanticizing" of the Catholic tradition. Aquinas tells of the ache in man's unfulfilled rationality which can be assuaged not by more truth but only by the

Truth.[45] For Lewis also, reason is the organ of truth. But for him imagination is the organ of *meaning,* which is the antecedent condition of both truth and falsehood.[46] The vehicle for meaning is metaphor and myth drawn from, and somehow conveying, the "romantic experience." "In the enjoyment of a great myth," Lewis argues, "we come nearest to experiencing as concrete what can otherwise be understood only as an abstraction."[47] And the "lovely falsehoods" of the poets, the myths, both ancient and modern, though false as history, "may be very near the truth as prophecy."[48] For the one who follows out the "dialectic of desire" the question eventually becomes (as it did for Lewis): "Where, if anywhere, have the hints of all Paganism been fulfilled?" And then, of course, one is confronted with the teaching of the incarnation.[49]

Even the gospel is myth, but it is "myth become fact." In Jesus Christ "the essential meaning of all things [comes] down from the 'heaven' of myth to the 'earth' of history"[50]—but, Lewis insists, "without ceasing to be myth." There is to be no demythologizing. "To be truly Christian we must both assent to the historical fact and also receive the myth (fact though it has become) with the same imaginative embrace which we accord to all myths."[51]

We can be assured—since there is "a kind of truth or rightness in the imagination itself"[52]—that whatever the imagination grasps as meaning will have some relevance to truth. But how can we know that we should in a special way accept this particular myth and assent to this particular historical fact, over against the many other myths and all the rest of history? As regards history, Lewis' answer is this: "On certain great events (those embodied in the creeds) we have what I believe to be divine comment which makes plain so much of their significance as we need, and can bear, to know."[53] As for the scriptural imagery, "it comes to us from writers who were closer to God than we, and it has stood the test of Christian experience down the centuries."[54] The basis for belief is, in a word, authority.

Now, it is easy to see—from this summary of Lewis' theological beliefs—where much of the dialogue and the commentary in the novels comes from and what the dialectic is according to which the characters are ranged with or against one another. But the analysis can go deeper yet—to account for certain characteristics of this fantasy and for certain failures in execution.

First of all, even Lewis' *use* of fantasy—his unique, apologetic use of it, with its double movement toward allegory and toward myth—may be related to his strong emphasis on the Godward side of the relation between Creator and creature. The emphasis on "beyondness" manifests itself in the dream framework and the heavenly setting of *The Great Divorce,* and in the involvement with the life on other planets in the trilogy. The insistence on objectivity is seen in the use of myth as "fact." The supernaturalism appears in our representatives in the novels encountering, not fellow human beings or even "humanoids," but creatures who are superhuman, who convey a sense of good (or evil) "otherness."

That these images relate also to some of the specific ideas of the Christian faith needs no further emphasis. It is interesting to note, however, how Lewis' special concern for the *praeparatio*—for helping man the creature to get ready for belief in God the Redeemer—affects the themes of the space trilogy. Since *Out of the Silent Planet* presents an image of the unfallen created order and *Perelandra* the temptation but with Paradise "retained" and *That Hideous Strength* the building and destroying of a modern, scientific Babel, it would seem that Lewis has confined himself, indeed, to the "beginnings."

This is not to say that Lewis' work shows unawareness of the modern sensibility. "All contemporary writers share to some extent the contemporary outlook," he once remarked, "even those, like myself, who seem most opposed to it."[55] But he is confident, as Farrer states, that we still have with us "a world haunted by the supernatural, a conscience haunted by the moral absolute, a history haunted by the divine claim of Christ."[56]

All these ideas or beliefs, I am saying, help to account for the "rhetoric," or "strategy," which we have seen developing. It is characterized by (1) *the deceptive surface* (quest journey, letters from hell, dream-vision, space journey, "fairy tale for grown-ups") with its double reference: to itself as fiction and to the pattern of ideas symbolized in it; (2) *the allegorical "pull,"* with its generally satiric intention, directed against false ideas; (3) *the reaching toward the mythic,* combining numinousness and facticity so as to convey the qualities of the objective Reality which is imaged; (4) *the dogmatic Christian base,* enabling the author to set up, by way of fantasy, analogues for certain objects of belief and examples of certain hindrances; (5) *the tendentious narrative technique,* by which the skeptical reader is encouraged to identify his ideas with those of an unbeliever in the world of the novel, only to find his "representative" moving toward belief.

The phrase "moving toward" is true, I think, to the immanent "intention" of these fictions. Lewis does not, in general, want to insist on full-blown belief; the minimum will do. Lewis tells us what happened to him when he chanced to read Macdonald's *Phantastes:* "It did nothing to my intellect nor (at that time) to my conscience. Their turn came far later and with the help of many other books and men. . . . What it actually did was to convert, even to baptize, . . . my imagination."[57] C. S. Lewis' literary apologetic is calculated to rehabilitate belief in supernaturalistic Christianity as a possibility for the modern sensibility; not to "confirm" the understanding—that can come later—but to "baptize" the imagination.

These convictions about transcendence and the supernatural help to account for much of the power of Lewis' work. But his *over-*emphases have something to do with the pervasive weaknesses. In style there is occasional overexplicitness and pseudoeloquence. Explicit allusions can become obtrusive. Lewis is trying to dramatize in his works the *content* of what he grasped in faith, as a convert, and to satirize specifically the things that stood in the way of his surrender. Perhaps, after all, he does find it difficult to confine himself merely to "baptizing" his reader's imagination; perhaps he wishes to "confirm" him as well.

Certain passages in Lewis' fiction can be seen as unfortunate attempts at the sublime, passages characterized by a piling up of images and by incantatory rhythm. Incantation is precisely what they are attempting. In one of his university sermons, after a lyrical exposition of the "romantic experience," Lewis suddenly stops and asks his congregation: "Do you think I am trying to weave a spell?" And he answers:

> Perhaps I am; but remember your fairy tales. Spells are used for breaking enchantments as well as for inducing them. And you and I have need of the strongest spell that can be found to wake us from the evil enchantment of worldliness which has been laid upon us for nearly a hundred years. Almost our whole education has been directed to silencing this shy, persistent, inner voice.[58]

The sudden irruption of such eloquence signals the reader that archetypes are lurking and the numinous is near. Why do these passages so often fail?

The problem seems to me to be one of belief. Lewis apparently entertains contradictory notions on the question of whether the romantic experience really *mediates* revelatory reality or merely *reflects* and points to a truth which has been revealed in another form. The more negative conclusion is most clearly stated in *Surprised by Joy:*

> I think that all things in their way, reflect heavenly truth, the imagination not least. "Reflect" is the important word. This lower life of the imagination is not a beginning of nor a step towards, the higher life of the spirit, merely an image.[59]

It may well be that what happens in these passages is that the *image* being evoked is incapable of arousing in the artist an imaginative intensity equal to the dogmatic conviction with which he holds the *belief* toward which it points and which it helps to convey. What purports to be mythopoeic is covertly allegorical; the myth is too thin, the allegory too thick. The eloquence, in short, is "insincere."

Second, there are lapses in tone. A cruel, vengeful note is heard in some satirical passages, and the images of the evils under attack are allowed to become grotesque. This is the case particularly in *The Pilgrim's Regress* and *That Hideous Strength,* where we often detect what G. S. Fraser has called the "coarse bullying tone" in Lewis. The source of these lapses I find in Lewis' low estimate of man, a certain disgust at man's creaturely limitations and his fallen wickedness.

The third weakness incorporates the other two, and goes further. The trouble with a good deal of Lewis' fantasy is its one-sidedness, its lack of a sufficient dialectical tension. The characters are puppets —obedient or enslaved creatures being used as instruments by more-than-human agencies or being suddenly overwhelmed by belief in the hitherto unbelievable. Professor Weston is made to seem almost incapable of anything good. The Lady on Perelandra is a figure in a preordained ritual. In *That Hideous Strength,* the representatives of Good and Evil (at St. Anne's and Belbury) are little more than symbolic figures. What of the skeptics who move toward belief, our "deputies" in the books? Ransom, in the first book of the trilogy, puts up practically no resistance; "Lewis" is present only in two chapters of *Perelandra;* the more "realistic" Studdocks of *That Hideous Strength* are, as I have already argued, unconvincing.

But in didactic literature two-dimensional characters abound. The problem has to do with the ideas which they represent or expound. If the unbeliever in each of us is to enter fully into the play of ideas by way of their fantastic images, there must be more of a sense of ideological combat than Lewis has created for us. Our "representatives" in these stories are the victims of an irresistible "grace." Speaking analogically again, the problem would seem to be the result, in part, of a "high" view of God, a "low" view of man, and an inadequate doctrine of incarnation. To put it bluntly, the manipulation of fantasy elements in his fiction (and this is true also for the "sophisticated" style in his apologetic writings) shows mainly Lewis' awareness that people do hold ideas about Christianity which are different from his, not his recognition that these ideas in themselves might have cogency.

With *Till We Have Faces,*[60] C. S. Lewis turns from the apologist's concern with the "other" to the autobiographical intent of his earliest fantasies. The nonfiction of Lewis' last years reveals a comparable shift of emphasis. *Surprised by Joy* (1955) is, of course, avowedly autobiographical. *A Grief Observed* (1961), torn from Lewis by the death of his wife (after a marriage of only three years), stands in startling contrast to the earlier, neatly organized, carefully argued treatise called *The Problem of Pain. Letters to Malcolm: Chiefly on Prayer* is, as the title suggests, epistolary in structure and informal in method. All these works, in comparison with the writings of the middle years, embody a deeper personal involvement with the subjects dealt with, a more "open" tone toward the reader, and a heightened dialectical tension in the setting forth of ideas.

The author's introductory note to *Till We Have Faces* suggests the depth of his involvement with its subject. It has lived in his mind, he says, "thickening and hardening with the years, ever since he was an undergraduate." Narrative technique also betrays that involvement. It is a first-person account, by Orual, the eldest daughter of Trom, king of Glome, of her dealings with the gods, "especially the god who lives on the Grey Mountain." The author is "closer" to this narrator-protagonist than he was to Ransom or the Studdocks in the trilogy. Judgment is still passed but with much more understanding and sympathy.

The apologetic intention is again present. The story is that of Orual's struggle against, and final surrender to, belief. It is—according to the "framing-device" at the end—particularly intended for the people of Greece. But *we* are "the Greeks"—represented in the story itself by Orual's teacher, a Greek slave named Lysias, nick-named "the Fox," who is a rationalist and a naturalist, the symbol of enlightenment. Even Lysias is not caricatured but is presented as a divided man, with some feeling for mystery. More centrally, however, we are Orual, still more divided than the Fox—desirous of learning from him to keep things "clear, hard, limited, and simple," and yet unable to shake off completely her superstitious terror of Ungit, the great goddess of Glome.

The movement of the novel is different, however, from what we have come to expect. We are not taken by magic from this actual, familiar world of ours to a real "other world" somewhere in Space. Instead, the action takes place at an indeterminate time in the distant past and in a vaguely intimated locale. No "Christians" appear in the story; and, if Christianity is present, it has to be by analogy only. C. S. Lewis, of course, is simply doing here what he understands Sidney to have done in the paganism of his *Arcadia*. "In such works the gods are God *incognito,* and everyone is in the secret. Paganism is the religion of poetry through which the author can express, at any moment, just so much or so little of his real religion as his art requires."[61]

Orual's story is—in the words of Lewis' prefatory note—a tale of "dark idolatry and pale enlightenment at war with each other and with vision, and the havoc which a vocation, or even a faith, works on human life." Its "plot," the subtitle reminds us, is that of a "myth retold," the myth of Cupid and Psyche and her envious sisters. Even as told or transmitted by Apuleius, in the second century, the story was considered an allegory of how the human soul is purified by sufferings and misfortunes and prepared for the enjoyment of true happiness. Lewis' theme is similar, but the changes he makes in the narrative reveal the differences in his conception of the process. His use of relatively sympathetic first-person narration, furthermore, brings us close to experiencing the movement from unbelief to belief, rather than merely contemplating the pattern of that process.

Orual, ugly but intelligent, has a sister named Redival who is pretty but empty-headed and vain. Into their lives comes a half sister, Istra (Psyche, in Greek), who grows up beautiful, bright, and joyous. Because of her beauty and goodness, Psyche is adored as if she were a goddess. This supposedly arouses the jealousy of Glome's Venus—black, faceless, stone Ungit. In Lewis' version of the story, famine and plague come upon the land, and Psyche is judged to be the Accursed One who is responsible for this. As such she is set apart to be given as the Great Offering to the "Brute." The Brute is understood also to be, in a mystery, Ungit, or Ungit's son, the god of the Mountain. It is important that in Lewis' story the god who loves Psyche is identical to what the people call the "Brute." Psyche has often expressed a strange longing for the Mountain, and she now welcomes her "marriage" to the god. But Orual, as she rides toward the Mountain after the Great Sacrifice, is in despair, sure she will find there only Psyche's remains.

The Fox, it becomes clear even this early, is "pale enlightenment," trying to explain away the "religious" beliefs about Ungit and the Brute. The worship of Ungit is "dark idolatry," the religion of fear, blood, mystery—but also of power. King Trom, for one, is not convinced by the Greek's rhetoric.

> "I, King, have dealt with the gods for three generations of men, and I know that they dazzle our eyes and flow in and out of one another like eddies on a river, and nothing that is said clearly can be said truly about them. Holy places are dark places. It is life and strength, not knowledge and words, that we get in them" [p. 50].

Psyche, then, is "vision," able to love the Truth which others over-simplify into clear and distinct ideas and the Reality which is concealed within the superstition. Because of her beauty and goodness, the antagonism she arouses, and the sacrifice she willingly becomes, she seems a kind of Christ. On the other hand, as Lewis himself suggests, perhaps she may best be understood as *anima naturaliter Christiana,* guided, but always in terms of her own imagination or that of her people, toward the true God.[62] She is ready to receive the coming truth, already adumbrating it in her attitudes and deeds. Orual is the one most at war—fascinated by yet fearing Ungit, drawn toward Greek enlightenment, and devoted to Psyche. Lewis makes the story hers, not Psyche's; and so we see *our* story as one, not of enlightened contemplation of truth or direct insight into mystery, but of disunion and conflict.

In a valley in the Mountain, Orual finds Psyche again, alive. Psyche claims really to have become the bride of a loving god and insists that they are standing at that moment in his palace. But Orual can see nothing of this; for her the palace is not there at all, and she thinks Psyche mad. The next morning, however, just as she is about to leave the Mountain, she has a glimpse of the god's dwelling. But the Fox, Orual herself, and others explain away that apparition and Psyche's "god." When Orual returns at a later time to the Mountain, it is in order to persuade, or force, Psyche to go back with her. First, however, Psyche must be brought to see what she has "married"; therefore, as in the original tale, we have the use of the lamp. At the moment when Psyche lights the lamp Orual sees the palace again, witnesses its sudden destruction, sees the god himself and the "passionless and measureless rejection" in his face, and hears him say: " 'Now Psyche goes out in exile. Now she must hunger and thirst and tread hard roads. Those against whom I cannot fight must do their will upon her. You, woman, shall know yourself and your work. You also shall be Psyche' " (pp. 173–74).

The invisibility of the palace is Lewis' "invention." Here, once again, the question is one of faith and sight, of belief and disbelief in the unseen but real supernatural. For Orual the fact that Psyche claims to see the palace while she cannot is "a sickening discord, a rasping together of two worlds, like the two bits of a broken bone"

(p. 120). But there is an even greater obstacle for her than the inability to believe what she cannot see. Her *will* is set against believing. To believe is to lose Psyche to the god, and her "love" for Psyche is a devouring passion which cannot endure the thought of giving her up, even to a god (Lewis wants us to think: *especially to a god*). The epigraph to the novel reads: "Love is too young to know what conscience is." But the next line in that Shakespearean sonnet is "Yet who knows not conscience is born of love?" The story now follows this development of "conscience" in Orual. She has seen the god ("My terror was the salute that mortal flesh gives to immortal things" [p. 171]), and she has heard the judgment on her ("You, woman, shall know yourself and your work" [p. 174]). Guilt, symbolized by the sound of weeping she often hears, hardens her. She resolves to accept her ugliness once and for all by always going veiled. She also perfects her swordsmanship, trained by the soldier Bardia.

Not long after, the king dies and she is made queen. Aided by her masculine toughness and by the mystery of her veil, and with Bardia and the Fox as her closest counselors, she reigns well for a number of years. Then one day in her old age, on a journey in a foreign land, she hears from a priest of that region a myth which turns out to be the story of Psyche, a tale in which the facts as Orual knows them have been greatly distorted. In her anger she decides to write the true account and to pour out her complaints against the gods, detailing all their unjust demands, their dark hints, and their lying stories. "Why must holy places be dark places?" she cries, and demands an end to ambiguity.

But when we turn the page, we find part 2; Orual is beginning it a few days later. This section, one quarter the length of part 1, is simply another version of the meaning of the events already narrated. New knowledge has come to Orual, and she must write again or die perjured. The knowledge has come partly by way of memory (The gods "used my own pen to probe my wound" [p. 254]) and partly through "strokes from without," including visions, or "seeings." She now realizes that she has always rejected her sister Redival and devoured—in her love-need—the time and strength of Bardia and the Fox. In one "seeing" she is brought by her father into a room deep below the Pillar Room and set before a mirror. As she stands there, she hears herself saying: "I am Ungit." That is, she is a thing all-devouring, womblike, yet barren. Glome is a web, and she the spider in its center. This is her "love."

In the last of the "seeings" she goes to appear, naked, before the gods to read her complaint. What she there sees before her is not a great book but "a little, shabby crumpled thing." When she attempts to read, she hears her own voice saying over and over sentences which simply expose her willful resistance to this "everlasting calling, calling, calling of the gods" and her jealousy of Psyche's love for them (pp. 289–92). She sees her complaint also for what it is, and warns:

> When the time comes to you at which you will be forced at last to utter the speech which has lain at the center of your soul for years, which you have, all that time, idiot-like, been saying over and over, you'll not talk about the joy of words. I saw well why the gods do not speak to us openly, nor let us answer. Till that word can be dug out of us, why should they hear the babble that we think we mean? How can they meet us face to face till we have faces? [p. 294].

The visions also reveal what Orual has been to Psyche and Psyche to her. She, and the others, have been "in league to keep a soul from being united with the Divine Nature" (p. 304). And yet she has also borne Psyche's anguish. The "seeings" have to do, we now realize, with the impossible tasks set for Psyche in the original story. They are Lewis' allegorical equivalents for sorting the grains, gathering the fleece, and obtaining the beauty of Proserpine. In all the tasks, Orual has labored and suffered; but she comes to recognize—in words she records in part 2—that Psyche "won without effort what utmost effort would not win for me" (p. 284). This is clearly not "justice": the gods are not "just." "What would become of us," asks the shade of the Fox, "if they were?" (p. 297). Orual instead receives more than justice. For now Psyche returns from the deadlands bringing "beauty in a casket from the Queen of the Deadlands, from death herself" to "make Ungit beautiful" (pp. 305–6).

It is, of course, Orual herself who is given the casket. She and Psyche stand together before a pool of clear water in a fair, grassy court. There the god appears—in unutterable splendor—to judge

Orual. She hears the great voice say: "You also are Psyche," and then sees in the water the reflections of two figures, both of them Psyches, "both beautiful . . . beyond all imaginings, yet not exactly the same" (p. 308). This is the last of Orual's "seeings" and very nearly the end of her life. She ends the second part also by addressing the gods—but with a difference.

> I ended my first book with the words *No answer*. I know now, Lord, why you utter no answer. You are yourself the answer. Before your face questions die away. What other answer would suffice? Only words, words; to be led out to battle against other words [p. 308].

What has Orual (and what have we) learned? The Fox, now eager (in the other world) to beg forgiveness for his glib and shallow dismissal of all things religious, has directed her to the truth in the worship of Ungit—that "there must be sacrifices. They will have sacrifice, will have men. Yes, and the very heart, center, ground, roots of a man; dark and strong and costly as blood" (p. 295). The ritual and myth of Ungit-worship is closer to Reality than is enlightened rationality, which writes off religion as "lies of the poets" and "not according to nature." Rationality, too, however, can put us on the way, as long as it remains open to mystery, to the gods which "dazzle our eyes and flow in and out of one another." But religion will remain "dark idolatry" and rationality will remain "pale enlightenment" unless each is joined with "vision." There is, it would seem, a direct way—Psyche's way—to the goal. But our way is always Orual's, the long way round. All "are born into the house of Ungit. And all must get free from her. Or say that Ungit in each must bear Ungit's son and die in childbed—or change" (p. 301). This is the "costingness of regeneration," the need for being unmade and remade so that Ungit can become Psyche and be united with the god.

We have been brought back to the theme of the soul's quest for God—more accurately, perhaps, the soul's quest for everything else but God, through which, somehow, the grace of God reveals to the soul that which it truly seeks. The direct way to God (Psyche) is sensed by fallen man only as an impossible possibility. Reason, unaided, can never reach God (the Fox, as he grew older, "seemed to be ever less and less a philosopher, and to talk more of eloquence, and figures, and poetry [p. 235]). Our way is the way of peremptory desire (Orual) oscillating between impure superstition (Ungit) and unchastened enlightenment (the Fox). The soul in this aspect loves the *experiencing* rather than the object *experienced*. It seizes on the medium through which the vision comes (Psyche) and loves it in place of, and even against, that which the vision beholds (the god). However, such misdirected love, through the pain it suffers and inflicts, awakens the moral sense ("Who knows not conscience is born of love?"). And so the soul moves through strenuous and joyless moral struggle toward the goal it seemingly should have reached much earlier, and directly ("We might have been two images of love," Orual notes, "the happy and the stern; she so young, so brightface, joy in her eyes and limbs; I, burdened and resolute, bringing pain in my hand" [p. 157]). But in the end it is seen that God, in his grace, has accepted the intention, no matter how obscured by self-love. By way of that moral effort—though not as its reward—a "face" has been prepared, an "I" by which the soul is enabled to receive the glory—though it is a different glory—glimpsed in the original vision.

This is an old story by now, this roundabout way back to the beginning. It is the "regress" again; it is the story which is made explicit in *Surprised by Joy*. In many respects *Till We Have Faces* also tells that story in the old way. In this last novel, as in the others, a "representative" appears whose point of view we share in the movement toward belief. Images of fantasy are presented in such a way as to pose the question of what is ultimately real. Again these images are given allegorical reference enriched and universalized toward mythic power. Much of that allegory draws our attention to the hindrances to faith, all that tends to "keep a soul from being united with the Divine Nature": superstition and idolatry, intellectualism, and (above all) self-centeredness. Analogies to Christian doctrine are worked out here as in the earlier fantasies. The Fox, in one of Orual's "seeings," prophesies a "far distant day when the gods become wholly beautiful, or we at last are shown how beautiful they always were" (p. 304). The qualities of the ultimate vision are suggested, once again, in passages of heightened or eloquent prose.

Some of the old weaknesses also reappear. Effective as the style of this novel generally is, a few of the passages that are meant to be most persuasive ring false. More seriously, though the novel convincingly presents Orual as the *struggling* soul, much of the imagery still suggests denigration of the human and excessive passivity in relation to "otherness." Orual, in part 3, is undergoing "the gods' surgery"; "those divine Surgeons," she writes, "had me tied down and were at work" (p. 266). In her vision of the fleece-gathering, she watches herself being trampled by the golden rams:

> They butted and trampled me because their gladness led them on; the Divine Nature wounds and perhaps destroys us merely by being what it is. We call it the wrath of the gods; as if the great cataract in Phars were angry with every fly it sweeps down in its green thunder [p. 284].

These, however, are relatively minor flaws. The most serious weakness makes itself apparent in the overall structure of the book. The first-person "complaint" of part 1 serves very well to set the questions, to express Orual's anguish, and to reveal her selfishness and pride. But Lewis seems to feel committed to the same technique for part 2, and there it is less effective. One can see him struggling with the problem of making Orual's last experiences "real." She is still in this life, yet she has to witness her final destiny. It would hardly do to present the experiences as mere dreams, and yet it is hardly possible to do anything else. "About this time," Orual writes, "there came (if you call it so) another dream. But it was not like a dream" (p. 283). And again: "What followed was certainly vision and no dream. . . . I walked into the vision with my bodily eyes wide open" (p. 285). One can also see the struggle to "get it all in." As a result, the succession of visions becomes clumsy and cluttered, so that the reader is likely to say, with Orual: "From this time onward they . . . drenched me with seeings" (p. 276).

These now familiar flaws in structure and style reflect the underlying continuity between the work of Lewis' middle period and the books produced in his last years. Just as important as the continuity, however, is the significant shift of emphasis revealed not only in the fiction but also in his other writings. In *Letters to Malcolm* Lewis seems less content to give merely dogmatic answers to existential questions. Lewis' own profound experience of pain seems to underlie many statements found in *Letters to Malcolm* as well as the whole of *A Grief Observed*. The Passion itself, he speculates at one point, may be—along with all the other things it is—the human situation writ large; what it means, in other words, to be a man. What, he asks, is the meaning of the last dereliction? "Is it that God Himself cannot be Man unless God seems to vanish at His greatest need?"[63]

The new spirit makes itself felt in the way Lewis tells his "old story" in *Till We Have Faces*. There is, first of all, a new acceptance of the split and the conflict as one's own burden. There is less of a tendency to despise what seem to be perversions of the vision and a greater willingness to accept these attitudes for what they are in themselves. This is shown by the universalizing (in contrast to the earlier satirical particularizing) of such elements. The writing conveys a deeper sense of the agony involved in the journey back, by such devious paths, to the original way—and it does so with less explicit reference to Christian dogma. Even the style seems to contribute to the universalizing of the vision, in its simplicity and flexibility in syntax, its unexpected "foreign-sounding" words and phrases, and its more restrained high points of eloquence.

What is to be said, finally, about the obvious power of Lewis' last fantasy in relation to the partial failure of the earlier work? Here I must dare to do what would have evoked Lewis' scorn—to espouse the "personal heresy," to look for the poet in the poem. I do so briefly, hesitantly, tentatively—and with the help of the recent *Light on C. S. Lewis,* written after his death by his friends and associates.

The question at this point is not so much *what* Lewis' beliefs were as *how* they were held. It may well be, first of all, that the signs of disunity in a good deal of his writing reveal the extremism toward which the thinking of the "twice-born" often tends. Austin Farrer may be right also in suggesting that C. S. Lewis was what he was partly because he came to Christian faith through philosophic idealism.[64] And Lewis himself spoke a number of times of a "split" within him between the claims of reason and those of imagination. In a poem called "Reason," he pleads for reconciliation:

> Oh who will reconcile in me both maid and mother,
> Who make in me a concord of the depth and height?
> Who make imagination's dim exploring touch
> Ever report the same as intellectual sight?
> Then could I truly say, and not deceive,
> Then wholly say, that I BELIEVE.[65]

There are grounds, then, it would seem, for asking the question Owen Barfield asked about his lifelong friend. Distinguishing between the "genius of the will" and that of the imagination, Barfield inquires: *"Was* there something, at least in his impressive, indeed splendid, literary personality, which was somehow—and with no taint of insincerity—*voulu?"*[66] The question is germane to what the analysis of Lewis' fantasy reveals: that at some points his strength lies in satire and at others in myth-making, that in both his writing at times shows signs of strain (of being "willed"), and that as a result most of his books, although they have "good things" in them, cannot sustain a total experience of unity and power.

What happens, then, in *Till We Have Faces* is that C. S. Lewis moves toward coming to terms with his own dividedness, even his "modernity." Do we dare to say that he moves toward becoming genuinely "incarnate" in his fantasy-creation? Lewis implies something like this in a poem so personal that one hesitates even to refer to it. Addressing his wife (of so few years), who is now dying, he writes:

> Only that now you have taught me (but how late) my lack.
> I see the chasm. And everything you are was making
> My heart into a bridge by which I might get back
> From exile, and grow man. And now the bridge is breaking.[67]

With *Till We Have Faces* Lewis may even have been coming to see his own concern with Christian apologetics as another example of the strenuousness with which we labor to prepare a "face" so that before the face of the god all questions can die away. A new "regress" may have been bringing him to an old realization—that (as Yeats once said) "we make out of the quarrel with others, rhetoric, but of the quarrel with ourselves, poetry."[68]

CHARLES WILLIAMS: FANTASY AND THE ONTOLOGY OF LOVE

CHAPTER 2

"The powerful exploration of power after his own manner"—this phrase is applied to the work of Peter Stanhope, the poet-playwright of Charles Williams' novel *Descent into Hell,* but it can be even better used as a descriptive label for Williams' own literary achievement. It has often been remarked that the novels of Charles Williams are explorations of power. One might even say that these novels— particularly the earlier ones, published in the early 1930's—are about *powers,* for they reveal Williams' special interest in the manipulation of occult forces, in the attempts to transcend the limitations of time and space, to control matter by means of mind, even to grasp at the key to the secrets of life and death.

In the first novel, *Shadows of Ecstasy,*[1] the concern is with the power *within* man. In the next four novels—*War in Heaven* (1930), *Many Dimensions* (1931), *The Place of the Lion* (1931), and *The Greater Trumps* (1932)—power is concentrated in objects or ideas which participate in some greater power and are amenable to the human imagination. Finally—in *Descent into Hell* (1937) and *All Hallows' Eve* (1945)—the locus of power shifts from the human individual and the magical object to human relationships, which in turn participate in the power of being itself.

The concept of power which is central to *Shadows of Ecstasy* is, as one of the characters of that novel phrases it, "the adaptation of the world to an idea of the world."[2] Nigel Considine, the central character, advocates "the transmutation of your energies, evoked by poetry or love or any manner of ecstasy, into the power of a greater ecstasy" (p. 83). The energy of love—whether disappointed or fulfilled—is to be turned inward so as to produce, through the power of the imagination, a new energy or ecstasy. Considine even presents the possibility that one may drive strength into the imagination of oneself as living so as to conquer death itself (Considine himself has taken one step toward this goal, being now two hundred years old). This positive program carries also a negative corollary, explicit opposition to two other supposed sources of power, reason and the Christian religion. What he has discovered supersedes reason and is the fulfillment of truth only dimly foreshadowed by Christ.

The person most drawn to Considine is a professor of applied literature, Roger Ingram, who feels himself to be alone in his reverence for the power that is in poetry. With him we learn that in Africa Considine has discovered the secret of power and has gained control over many people, now his devotees—a control which is exerted over the entire consciousness except for the "secret center" and the mere exterior apprehension of the world. The dialectic which is being worked out in the lives of those persons who have come to know Considine operates at the international level in the "invasion" of England by Considine's Africans. This is in fact merely a small landing and an air raid, and its function is primarily to cause panic; but before its collapse it almost achieves a wider success. Africa, then, is the symbol of the natural energies, the possibility of ecstacy, and stands over against European civilization, which tends to suppress even the "shadows" of that ecstacy, poetry and romantic love.

In certain respects *Shadows of Ecstasy* is typical of Williams' fiction. The subject is power, power connected in some way with the exercise of the imagination. That central energy is related to imaginative literature, romantic love, and the religious enterprise. Each kind of response to the manifestation of power is embodied in a figure and in the developing action, so that both plot and characterization are governed by the idea and its dialectical unfolding. The power is shown, moreover, to be supernatural, through the use of elements of fantasy that transcend everyday probability.

In the next four novels[3] the focus is not only on the energy of the human imagination but also on certain objects, creatures, and rituals which become centers of power. The "war in heaven" is fought, on its earthly front, over the Holy Grail, which has turned up in the sacristy of Julius Davenant, archdeacon of Castra Parvulorum, also known as Fardles. The enemy is a retired publisher named Gregory Persimmons, who dabbles in the occult—making use of a magical ointment, a death-dealing diagram, an attempt at transference of souls between a dead man and a living one, and the esoteric rite of the Black Mass.

Another ancient object of power, a stone from the crown of Solomon, has the "many dimensions" of Williams' next title. This stone is supposedly First Matter, out of which all spirits and material things are made. Under the will of a single mind the stone makes possible the overleaping of spatial and temporal limitation and the entering of other minds.

In *The Place of the Lion* an escaped lioness has become, through the intense concentration of an occultist named Berringer, an opening whereby the Principles or Ideas or Archetypes of things can begin to draw their material ectypes back into that other, transcendental world. The world of particulars is preserved through the intervention of Anthony Durrant, who, playing Adam, reinvokes through naming them the material things which are being subsumed into their eternal Forms.

The cards in *The Greater Trumps,* the one perfect Tarot deck, along with the table of moving golden figures which match them, are in correspondence with the universe. The four suits control the elements and the humors; the Greater Trumps hold the secrets of the principles of thought and existence, "the meaning of all process and the measure of the everlasting dance" (*GT,* p. 20). Through their efficacy a fierce snowstorm is raised and then dissipated, and the "golden cloud of the beginning of things" is released and then recalled.

In all these books our attention is meant to be drawn chiefly to those persons who become vehicles for the essential goodness of the power centered in the magical objects and acts. "Vehicles" is just what they are; the Archdeacon exhorts his companions: "Make yourselves paths for the Will of God" (*WIH,* p. 156). The passive role is made easier by virtue of the fact that the "saviors" are such ordinary persons. The earthly "general" for the "war in heaven" is a little archdeacon in an obscure rural parish. The path for the power of the Stone is provided by Chloe Burnett, a secretary. Anthony

Durrant, the Adam who re-creates a world threatened with dissolution, is the subeditor of a minor journal. Nancy Coningsby, who learns to control the Greater Trumps, is merely the daughter of an unimportant legal officer.

These persons, and the others who aid them against the misuses of power, approach that ultimate power by way of various images, the "shadows of ecstasy." When the Duke of the North Ridings joins the Archdeacon in the Grail-vigil, his thoughts are of the kingly and priestly functions of those who have adored the consecrated chalice (*WIH*, p. 152). Lord Arglay, Chloe's employer and fellow servant of the Stone, is Chief Justice, but, Williams tells us, he wants to *"become justice"* (*MD*, p. 52). Anthony represents the true life of learning, in contrast to the pseudoknowledge of Damaris Tighe; she merely *uses* the intellect, whereas Anthony thinks of philosophy as something greater than his own mind. For several people in these novels poetry is the conductor of energy. The Archdeacon adores the ultimate Power as he performs his ecclesiastical duties, and the ritual of the church becomes prominent in the patterns of imagery not only in *War in Heaven* but also in the Christmas Day service described in *The Greater Trumps*.

There is also, however, another way to the power, the interior journey of the mystic. Archdeacon Davenant is somewhat inclined toward that way, and so is Nancy's Aunt Sybil. In fact, at the end of *The Greater Trumps* the preservation of the world comes about because "the search within and the search without [have been] joined" (*GT*, p. 267). The strongest proponent of the *via negativa*, however, is the bookstore assistant in *The Place of the Lion*, the young man called Richardson.

> Not by books or by phrases, not by images or symbols or myths did he himself follow . . . [the Way]. He abstracted himself continually from sense and from thought, attempting always a return to an interior nothingness where that which is itself no thing might communicate its sole essential being [*POL*, p. 157].

But this is not the way followed by the central characters. They affirm the power of goodness and the goodness of the ultimate power by way of particular pursuits, such as poetry, politics, or priestcraft. One avenue becomes increasingly important, that of relationships—of friendship or romantic love. Anthony, for example, learns that right knowledge of the great Principles of things is possible by friendship and love; that whereas much is possible to a man in solitude, some things—especially that "balance" which includes the virtues of humility and lucidity—are possible only in companionship (*POL,* pp. 213-14). He thus becomes a vehicle not merely for power as such but for the power of love. It is in *The Greater Trumps,* especially, that romantic love is represented as essential to the resolution of the conflict. Nancy learns that the everlasting dance of which the Greater Trumps are the measure is love. Henry Lee, who has come to love her, says:

> "All things are held together by correspondence, image with image, movement with movement. Without that there could be no relation and therefore no truth. It's our business—especially yours and mine—to take up the power of relation" [*GT,* p. 47].

The transmutation of energies, the mana of the Grail, the Stone with the inscribed Tetragrammaton, the recalling of the material world beginning at "the place of the lion," the releasing of the creative and destructive powers of the Tarots—these are now seen as mere images by which Williams explores a greater power, the power of being as such. Charles Williams is, one might say, an ontologist.

The phrase "mere image" fails, however, to suggest the depth of Williams' interest in the occult. For a time Williams was even associated with the Order of the Golden Dawn, a hermetic order founded by Rosicrucians and inclined toward experimentation in various of the occult arts. Other literary figures influential on Williams, such as W. B. Yeats, A. E. Waite, and Arthur Machen, also belonged at one time or another to the group.[4] Nominally, Williams remains carefully noncommittal about the claims of occultism. His statement about witchcraft summarizes the possibilities:

> Some have supposed that it had no identity in itself, that its image was only a reflection of man's desire and man's capacity; others have thought that the image was of an actual being, allied to men only in the sense that men are spirit, differing from men in the sense that men are matter and that it is not, and never can be, matter.[5]

Yet in the Arthurian poems he posits a potentiality of being, symbolized by the forest called Broceliande, which lies beyond everyday probability and normal human consciousness. One is reminded of Paul Tillich's ontology, where the recognition of an aspect of being lying beneath "the split into universal essences and particular contents" makes possible for Tillich, too, a more positive attitude toward the symbolic power and value, not only of "nature" but also of the human body and even of such entities—beloved of occultists—as numbers, light, precious stones, and the four elements.[6]

Williams seems to assume, then, that the explorers of the occult do have access to this region of possibilities, so that their activity is, at worst, a distortion of the true supernatural and not merely an expression of man's desire and man's capacity. He tends, in any case, to exalt the objective at the expense of the subjective. What a skeptic such as Lord Arglay has to come to is not self-understanding but a belief in something outside himself. Recalling certain moments of profound repose experienced after doing his best for a good purpose, he wonders "whether that profound repose was not communicated from some far source and whether the life that is in it was altogether governed by time" (*MD*, p. 113).

Charles Williams, in short, is a thoroughgoing supernaturalist. He predicates modes of existence other than those perceived by the senses and known by reason and takes for granted that the natural order proceeds from and is dependent upon a reality which is invisible and which operates by laws transcending those discoverable in the visible world. He is eager to insist, however, that the supernatural is not divorced from the natural; one is not to escape from sensory illusion into spiritual reality. It is rather the true form of the natural, so that one knows the supernatural through images within the natural. Shakespeare, says Williams, conceived the whole supernatural life in terms of the natural, and his work should stand as a rebuke to "arrogant supernaturalists."[7]

Williams is also—in a special sense of the word—a romanticist. That is, he holds that there are certain "natural" experiences which can image for us the transcendent Good. The "romantic experience" is related to the idea of magic and, along with magic, to the power of being as such. The predisposition toward the idea of magic can arise in either of two ways. What both have in common is that they overthrow a simple trust that phenomena are what they seem. That predisposition may arise out of the "moment when it seems that anything might turn into anything else" or out of those moments when "a phenomenon [not about to alter] but being wholly itself, is laden with universal meaning. A hand lighting a cigarette is the explanation of everything; a foot stepping from a train is the rock of all existence."[8]

Such an experience, the novels imply, can flow from the reading of great poetry, the life of learning, the dispensing of authority and justice, or the ritual of the church. There are other avenues as well, such as nature and (the one most traveled in Williams' work) romantic love. Williams places himself in the tradition of Dante, Donne, Coventry Patmore, and even that "salutary heretic" D. H. Lawrence, in the development of what Mary M. Shideler has called "the theology of romantic love." The shock of the moment which (with Dante in mind) Williams calls "Beatrician" puts a man under an obligation to explore the implications—particularly the theological implications—of that access of power.

But if the goal for man is to know the power of being, and with a knowledge which approaches union, then there is also another way entirely, the *via negativa* seen in the mysticism of Richardson in *The Place of the Lion.* In *The Descent of the Dove,* his idiosyncratic history of the church, Williams insists on the coexistence of the two ways:

> The one Way was to affirm all things orderly until the universe throbbed with vitality; the other to reject all things until there was nothing anywhere but He. The Way of Affirmation was to develop great art and romantic love and marriage and philosophy and social justice; the Way of Rejection was to break out continually in the profound mystical documents of the soul, the records of the great psychological masters of Christendom. All was involved in Christendom, and between them, as it were, hummed the web of the ecclesiastical hierarchy.[9]

God is *known* by the affirmation of images, known to be *God* by their rejection. That is the point of the epigram "This also is Thou; neither is this Thou" which appears so often in Williams' writings. Idolatry is an ever-present danger. Though for romantic theology

C

the beloved is the first preparatory form of heaven and earth, for superstition heaven and earth are seen reduced to the form of the beloved. Acknowledging this danger of a false devotion, Williams still insists, however, that "unless devotion is given to a thing which must prove false in the end, the thing that is true in the end cannot enter."[10]

The ontology implied in the novels of Charles Williams is sacramentalist. Being is manifested in two modes, spiritual and material. It is not even, Williams wants to insist, that the spiritual *uses* the physical; there is a common, even a single, operation.[11] Williams can assert all that the sacramental view of the universe asserts:

> the supremacy and absolute freedom of God; the reality of the physical world and its process as His creation; the vital significance of the material and temporal world to the eternal Spirit; and the spiritual issue of the process in a fellowship of the finite and time-enduring spirits in the infinite and eternal Spirit.[12]

What authenticates this union of physical and spiritual is the incarnation. "He who is *Theos* is *Anthropos* and all the images of *anthropos* are in him."[13] In his theological writings Williams is always careful to repudiate what he calls the "unofficial Manichaeism" of our time and to insist that the principle of our sensuality is unique and divine. He is particularly emphatic on this point since he inclines toward the belief—chiefly associated with the name of Duns Scotus—that the incarnation would have taken place even had there been no fall, that "Incarnation is the point of creation."[14]

At certain points Williams is at pains to stress the historicity of the incarnation, the absolute newness of what happened in the life of Jesus of Nazareth. In the play "The Death of Good Fortune" he has Mary say:

> Incipit vita nova: substance is love,
> love substance. Begins substance to move
> through everywhere the sensuality of earth and air.
> I was its mother in its beginning.[15]

But—as even this passage reveals—he is usually more concerned with universality of meaning than with particularity of event. The incarnation tells the secret truth about creation. The inseparability of "sensuality" and "substance," of flesh and spirit, seen in the incarnate Christ is in the creation "a natural fact as well as a supernatural truth."[16]

That "natural fact," inherent in creation and manifested in incarnation and continually reaffirmed in sacrament, is what Williams calls the coinherence. By coinherence he means, of course, relationship; but he also includes mutuality, reciprocity, exchange. "We may or may not live *for* others, but whether we like it or not, we do live *from* others."[17] Coinherence is manifested at all levels, or in all modes, of existence. There is interchange between matter and spirit, producing the "correspondences" of the occult arts and symbolist poetry. Within the individual person there is interchange between body and spirit: "flesh knows what spirit knows, but spirit knows it knows."[18] The human body can be, in Wordsworth's phrase, "an index of delight" (*Prelude,* book 8, lines 276–78).

Williams has much to say also about the necessary coinherence of the sensual and the intellectual. His is a corrected romanticism which holds to the sacredness of "fact" and the requirement of "accuracy." The ideal is not spontaneous feeling nor rigid rationality but the "feeling intellect." Similarly, in the practical realm order is to be imposed on the flux of natural moods and passions, so as to produce virtue, courtesy, intelligence, and ritual. The law of coinherence is descriptive and prescriptive, ultimately, for the material dimension, the human reality, social relationships, and imaginative creation. Even metaphysical principles—freedom and necessity, for instance, or the One and the Many—may be seen, in the last analysis, as coinherent.

There are three distinctive modes of coinherence.

1. *Economic and political exchange.* This has to do with goods and services. Natural law obtains; man's duty and privilege is to accept freely his rightful place in a republican and yet hierarchical order of creation.
2. *Exchange between persons.* This can take place in the sexual relation of marriage, in other forms of love, in friendship, and in the priestly function. Theologically this is the sphere of the incarnation.

3. *The vision of universal coinherence.* Here we approach the mystery of the Divine Life itself.[19]

All those who recognize the coinherence and who live by exchange are citizens of the kingdom—which Williams more often calls the Republic, or the City. The City subsumes all the modalities of exchange: economic, political, ecclesiastical, personal. It both exists in its various particular societies and images the eternal web. Its coming is both contemporary and future, and its structure is at once hierarchic and republican. As such it incarnates the mode of being of the Trinity itself, three "persons" possessing "co-inherence in one another without any coalescence or commixture."[20]

Even the notion of individuality, then, requires ultimately for its explication the notion of coinherence, since "relationship, like separation, is an ultimate metaphysical reality and the substantial basis for being."[21] To refuse the coinherence, then, is to separate oneself from the "nature of things." To accept it is to believe in the power of being and to participate aright in that power—for power is not something one has but something one is. It is, finally, to believe that the ultimate nature of that power of being is Love, and to become a vehicle for that Love.

In the earliest novels Williams concerns himself with appearance and reality and with the possibility of so dealing with the world of appearances that one will know the power and the glory of that reality. The epigram attributed to Hermes Trismegistus might well be written over these works: "As above, so below." Even the titles suggest this: *Shadows of Ecstasy, War in Heaven, Many Dimensions.* To recall once again the words of Henry Lee to Nancy Coningsby,

> "All things are held together by correspondence, image with image, movement with movement. Without that there could be no relation and therefore no truth. It is our business—especially yours and mine—to take up the power of relation" [*GT*, p. 47].

The earliest novels "take up the power of relation" between material and spiritual reality; all existence is correspondence.

But the parenthetical phrase "especially yours and mine" is significant of a change of emphasis. For Nancy and Henry are in love, and they are exploring the power not only of correspondence but of coinherence. The invokers of power in the first three books work, in a sense, alone. They may have support and assistance, but they do not call upon the power in the name of that relationship. By contrast, when Nancy, along with Henry, handles the Tarots on Christmas Eve, she is consciously "inviting a union between the mystery of her love and the mystery of the dance" (*GT*, p. 105). At such a moment one can know himself to be—in a play on words found often in Williams' writings—*in* Love; one can have a sense of living within the beloved, of loving from the great web itself.[22] The Beatrician moment images, and participates in, the supernatural fact of coinherence; all existence is relationship.

In a discussion of "the achievement of the Grail," Williams recalls that for Dante human beatitude entailed an understanding of the incarnation, whereas for Angela of Foligno it meant knowing how God comes into the sacrament. Williams accepts both requirements, but he also calls upon us to live *in* these truths and *beyond* them, being "conscious of them as one is conscious of oneself, Christ-conscious instead of self-conscious."[23] But the word beyond seems to point to the ultimate vision of coinherence, to the *visio dei* itself. Being itself is Love, existence is adoration. In their exploration of the power of correspondence and the power of relationship, the novels of Charles Williams ultimately—in the words of the hymn which so strikes Nancy Coningsby's imagination—"rise to adore the mystery of love" (*GT*, pp. 122 ff.).

To refuse coinherence is, I have said, to separate oneself from "the nature of things." But that refusal can be made, has been made, and is being made by men everywhere. The emphasis on this fact helps to make Charles Williams' last two novels so different from the earlier ones. The same refusal is found there too, of course, but only in characters of secondary importance. With *Descent into Hell*,[24] however, as the title indicates, the process of damnation in a man capable of good is set forth as the central theme.

But there is something else in these last books which constitutes a new element in Williams' fiction; it concerns the nearness and continuing power of those who are dead. This becomes a means whereby the author can suggest a coinherence not only of the natural with the more-than-natural, but also of death with life and of past (dead) time with the living present. The setting for *Descent into Hell,* Battle Hill, is a place of the dead. A Protestant peasant named Struther (an ancestor of Pauline Anstruther) was burned there during the reign of Mary Tudor; a Jesuit was hunted down in Elizabeth's time; and a workman hanged himself in Lawrence Wentworth's house a few years before the onset of the novel's action. Struther and the workman are the two "amphibia" who not only haunt Battle Hill but become involved in the lives of those now living there.

As for the last novel, *All Hallows' Eve,*[25] we are in the realm of the dead from the very beginning; in fact, the story is told largely from the point of view of Lester Furnival, who, with her school chum, Evelyn Mercer, has just been killed. Much of that story, moreover, concerns the efforts of the sorcerer Simon Leclerc to traffic with the dead.

Even with these changes, coinherence remains the theme, and images are still drawn largely from the occult. But in these novels there has been a further development along the lines already traced, an emphasis on interchange within the human person and in personal relations rather than on correspondences seen in, and by way of, things. The individual is taken to be an indissoluble, co-inherent unity, "the very body of the very soul that are both names of the single man" (*DIH,* p. 28). The dwarf woman fashioned by the magic of Simon Leclerc falls short of true life, we are told, because it is a false incarnation, a coherence but not a coinherence (*AHE,* p. 201).

The image of the City is often evoked in both books. Lester, in the world of the newly dead, has a vision of the City—the earthly analogue of the coinherent life of the Trinity—and realizes that there citizenship means relationship (*AHE,* pp. 188–89). Negatively, the workman of *Descent into Hell* has hanged himself, we are told, because the Republic betrayed him. In these novels, especially, Williams seeks to convey the sense of an *ontology* of relationship. The "frame" for the events of *Descent into Hell* is the preparation for

and performance of a play, written mainly for the cultured ladies of
the Battle Hill community by the talented poet Peter Stanhope. But
even this play is clearly intended as a symbolic equivalent of universal coinherence; it is a communication of "the condition and . . .
the air of supernatural life . . . the incantation and adoration of the
true substance of experience" (*DIH,* p. 167).

Reference is also made in these novels to various forms of the
"romantic experience." The "entwined loveliness" of Stanhope's
verse is to Pauline Anstruther a mirror of the world's being (*DIH,*
p. 100). For Richard Furnival, his wife, Lester, has become in death
his Beatrice—"all known things similes of her; and beyond all
known things the unknown power of her" (*AHE,* p. 48). But one
also encounters here the negative romantic experience, the angst,
even the sense of "outrage," as Williams often calls it, which can be
aroused by the realization that the goodness of being may, at the
very heart of things, stand confronted by an ultimate contradiction.

For Pauline the terror of this experience is bound up with the
appearances—more and more frequent in recent years—of her
Doppelgänger. To her neighbor Lawrence Wentworth, the military
historian, the "outrage" has come in a different form. His self-
esteem as a historian has been threatened by the growing reputation
of a certain Aston Moffatt. His bachelor's solitude has been invaded
by dreams and fantasies concerning Adela Hunt, who is young and
vivacious and fancies herself "the leader of the younger artistic
party" in Battle Hill.

In Pauline and Wentworth two aspects of Williams' notion of
evil and sin are seen. The belief in coinherence and the way of
affirmation of images will sooner or later require a person to affirm
as good what seems to entail nothing but suffering and loss. Williams' other works, especially the plays, emphasize the terror which
is inseparable from the love that is ultimate, the evil out of which
good must often come. An enigmatic figure, the Skeleton in *Thomas
Cranmer of Canterbury,* calls himself "the delator of all things to
their truth" and "the Judas who betrays men to God." Contradiction
is found not just over against the good but (apparently) within the
good. We cannot act without committing or suffering "outrage."

"Nothingness" is a positive and powerful thing; yet, Williams reminds us, our Lord entered this nothingness too, and when we confront it we confront him. We must choose, then, whether to love or to hate that necessity which, properly known, is love.[26]

Pauline Anstruther's fears have to do with a contradiction which is felt to be, so to speak, outside her, an evil apparently within existence itself. The contradiction in Wentworth is within his will; it is sin. For sin is, essentially, a wrong mode of knowing. As Williams' reading of the Garden of Eden story would imply, the contradiction in man lies in the fact not that he knows good and evil but that—all being good—he both knows good and knows good *as evil*.[27] The latter knowledge, according to C. S. Lewis' interpretation of Williams' Arthurian poems, includes knowledge of those contingent things which God knew but would not create and which Adam insisted on experiencing. Evil, then, is felt not as imperfection, not even as revolt, but as *miscreation,* the bringing to pass of what cannot—and must not—be, but somehow is.[28]

For Williams sin always involves a failure of intellect as well as of will. Wentworth willfully rejects the opportunity for unselfish joy at the knighting of Aston Moffatt and becomes jealous of "his" Adela and her Hugh Prescott. In both instances he fails to know the truth as good. He now begins to lose his hold on truth as such; he twists evidence, surrenders his fidelity to fact. Meanwhile, with the aid of Stanhope and her grandmother Margaret Anstruther, to whom she is acting as companion, Pauline resolves to face and accept her apparitions.

Aware of the doubleness of existence, Stanhope is able to affirm its ultimate beauty and goodness ("He himself said, in reply to an interviewer's question, that he was an optimist and hated it" [*DIH,* p. 4]). He instructs Pauline in the special way of dealing with contradiction which is called substitution. One result of the negative romantic experience is a fundamental confusion concerning appearance and reality. The way to the truth, Stanhope tells her, is not the exercise of the imagination on the contents of one's own consciousness, nor is it the magical invocation of the power of Being. It is rather the exercise of mutuality; it is exchange, not just as a fact to be assented to but as an act of the will. It is the practical affirmation of coinherence in the face of the experience of contradiction. Stanhope offers, in short, to carry her burden of fear for her; he will take it up by a deliberate act of substituted love, and she will be able to look upon her shadow self without the usual terror. Since it is a fact that we live *from* one another, we can also resolve to be "obedient to the whole fixed nature of things" and live *for* one another (*DIH*, p. 107).

Having known peace for the first time in many years, Pauline determines to build her life around the principle of substituted love. By this time she has come to realize that the horror of her "double" is somehow bound up with the painful death centuries ago of her ancestor John Struther. Her grandmother, nearing death, senses in a kind of vision that someone out on the Hill is in need of Pauline's help. Pauline goes out into the darkness and not far from Wentworth's house sees a figure swaying and gesticulating in agony, calling out: "Lord God, I cannot bear the fear of the fire." She tries to say the words that will help, but cannot. Then behind her she hears: "Give it to me, John Struther." It is her own voice that has spoken; and, as she turns, Pauline sees her double, but sees her now as a "glorious creature," burning and glowing, "bright as if mortal flesh [has] indeed become what all lovers know it to be" (*DIH*, pp. 186–90). The thing she has always feared she now sees to be her true, hidden, glorious self; the terror which she has always felt turns out to be John Struther's fear, which she has carried without knowing or accepting it. Thus, Williams tells us, "it had been her incapacity for joy, nothing else, that had till now turned the vision of herself aside; her incapacity for joy had admitted fear, and fear had imposed separation" (*DIH*, p. 191). Now, having actively affirmed existence as the "terrible good" that it is, she has been reborn in love and joy; Struther's cry is hers also—"I have seen the salvation of my God."

Lawrence Wentworth, however, refuses to affirm the facts as good; he refuses coinherence. He declines to accept the help, or even acknowledge the full presence, of any "other"; it is good, he is coming to believe, for man to be alone. In response to his wishes, his imagination enables him, so to speak, to reenact Eden. As Adam he rejects his "Eve," the other, and chooses Lilith instead. According to the legends, Williams writes elsewhere, Lilith, the daughter of Samael the accursed, was the first wife of Adam and symbolizes "the idea of the woman of the darkness who loves and kills."[29] Wentworth creates his own "Adela," a projection of his desires, and makes love to this magical creature. "Image without incarnation, it was the delight of his incarnation, for it was without any of the things that troubled him in the incarnation of the beloved" (DIH, p. 139). Whereas Pauline Anstruther is haunted by a wraithlike figure that she does not want to see, and learns finally to see it as an image of her true self, Lawrence Wentworth invokes the shadow that he prefers to reality and finally can no longer evade its unreality.

Wentworth has fallen victim to one of Hell's attacks on Romantic love. There are three such false possibilities. One may believe that such an experience is everlasting, not realizing the need for nurturing its fruits by the exercise of charity and humility. One may believe that the experience is sufficient, limiting love to the moment of vision alone. Or—and this is most common in Williams' novels —one may make the experience exclusively personal.[30] Central to all these expressions of sin is the "preference of an immediately satisfying experience of things to the believed pattern of the universe."[31] But that pattern is one of coinherence; so that once again sin is to be seen not only as a failure to will the good but as an unwillingness to know the good, as good. Those who choose to know it falsely, as evil, dwell in illusion, "the opposite of holy fact, and the contradiction of sacred love" (DIH, p. 227).

But this is to choose Hell—hell being for Williams a fact of this life, certainly, if not also of some other mode of existence. Wentworth's descent is presented symbolically in what is at first a dream, later a waking fantasy, of climbing down a shining white rope. The rope also becomes a means for establishing the parallel between Wentworth and the workman who hanged himself in what was later Wentworth's house. The scholar's sin is pride, the workman's was despair: "The self-worship of the one was the potential source of cruelty, as the self-loathing of the other was the actual effect of cruelty; between them lay all the irresolute vacillations of mankind, nourishing the one and producing the other" (*DIH*, p. 145).

There is no peace for Lawrence Wentworth. Not satisfied in the embraces of the false incarnation of love, he is also repelled by the crude actuality of the real Adela. He can no longer work efficiently; he goes out less often, refusing even to evaluate responsibly some sketches for uniforms to be used in the play. Gradually even everyday reality begins to become unreal. His final rational undertaking is a trip to London for a gathering of historical scholars, a supper which Williams seems to intend as a secular image of the eucharist, but which becomes for Wentworth not a saving communion but a final isolation. He is descending into a Dantean darkness, toward the antithesis of love; he has seen, Peter tells Pauline, "the Gorgon's head that was hidden from Dante in Dis" (*DIH*, p. 239).

At the supper he meets Aston Moffatt. It is his last chance for fidelity to the truth. But he looks at his rival and thinks, not "He was wrong in his facts," but "I've been cheated." At that point all becomes meaningless, even the faces and conversation around him. The rope is gone now, and he is drawn "steadily, everlastingly, inward and down through the bottomless circles of the void" (*DIH*, pp. 247–48).

All Hallows' Eve takes up again several of the ideas prominent in *Descent into Hell;* in certain other respects it is reminiscent of the earlier novels. The evil figure who calls himself Father Simon is seeking to plumb the mysteries by means of magic and witchcraft. He insists on reserving power to himself rather than giving of himself and his power for others; he uses power, instead of contemplating and adoring it and its source. But, in addition, he refuses to be a mere vehicle of power, refuses to *receive* power, in the measure ordained. He wants to be *sicut deus* in every respect, self-empowered and self-existent rather than dependent, not only knowing good and evil but also having the power of life and death.

This intelligent, ascetic master of magic has set himself—in contrast with "that other child of a Jewish girl"—to "decline pain and ignorance" (*AHE*, p. 120). To some extent he has even transcended temporal limitation, for he has been alive for several centuries. He has taken a step also toward omnipresence, using a magic mirror to create two other images of himself who are now proclaiming his message of peace and love in other parts of the world. He refuses even to acknowledge the boundary between life and death. Just as the ancient sorcerer Simon Magus, according to legend, had slain a boy by magic and sent his soul to serve him in the spiritual places (since the soul, free from the body, acquires prescience), this Simon, too, plans to assert his lordship over the realm of the dead and be worshiped there.

The emissary is to be Betty Wallingford, the daughter of Simon Leclerc and Lady Wallingford. Betty is dominated and demeaned by her mother and exploited by Simon. Already he is sending her for short periods of time into the region of the newly dead to bring him news of what is to come. Her one hope is the love of the young painter Jonathan Drayton. Jonathan's suspicions about Father Simon are also felt by his best friend, Richard Furnival, whose wife, Lester, is already in that realm which Betty is exploring from time to time. The traffic between the living and the dead is even more integral to this novel than to *Descent into Hell*. Not only does the action of the novel begin with the newly dead Lester and Evelyn but, more importantly, the decisive actions are performed by the dead on behalf of the living. Here, as in *Descent into Hell,* these are acts of substituted love, issuing in salvation.

What is new in this novel, however, is the emphasis on repentance and forgiveness. Coinherence must be affirmed not only in the face of general suffering and loss but also in the face of personal wrongs done or suffered. In *All Hallows' Eve* the memories that Lester and Richard have of their marriage lead them both to repentance of their egotism, so that even across the frontier between life and death all is set right between them. The reader also witnesses Lester's repentance for long-ago injuries to Betty Wallingford's feelings, in contrast to Evelyn's insistence on clinging to her hate and malice. Since repentance is "a passionate intention to know all things after the mode of heaven,"[32] Betty's ungrudging offer of forgiveness is a means for redeeming the past into love.

Such pardon and such reconciliation, however, are costly. Any violation of coinherence inflicts a wound and leaves scars. This is true, in a mysterious way, for God himself. We have already noted that Williams is inclined to say (with Irenaeus and Duns Scotus) that "the world exists for the Incarnation rather than the Incarnation for the world." But, since man exercised his freedom to know good as evil, "the Incarnation became the Redemption for the sake of the world."[33] God elected both to put up with man's choice as Creator and to endure it as Victim. It is precisely on the basis of that act of substituted love that he has set up the new relationships of redemption. A man is enabled to know all things as occasions of love not simply through the affirmation of particular things as images of the absolute good, but even more centrally by the embracing of that symbol of ultimate contradiction, the Cross.

> By that central substitution, which was the thing added by the Cross to the Incarnation, He became everywhere the center of, and everywhere He energized and reaffirmed, all our substitutions and exchanges. He took what remained, after the Fall, of the torn web of humanity in all times and places, and not so much by a miracle of healing as by a growth within it made it whole. Supernaturally he renewed our proper nature.[34]

The secret truth about man as creature is his participation in the coinherent web of being-as-good. The manifest truth about him is coinherence in sin. "I have wondered," Williams speculates, following Augustine, "if indeed we were not all there, if all mankind was not then simultaneous and coinherent, and whether all mankind did not then choose amiss."[35] But the atonement is also a cosmic fact. "The central mystery of Christendom," we are told in *Descent into Hell,* "the terrible fundamental substitution, . . . shewed not as a miraculous exception, but as the root of a universal rule" (*DIH,* p. 211). If the primal requirement for man is to be "obedient to the whole fixed nature of things," the opportunity for those who have recognized and repented of their coinherence in Adam is to be obedient to the renewed nature of things in the atonement. Acts done in union with that act have a unique validity.

The costliness of that act and of its reenactments is often represented in Williams' novels. Margaret Anstruther, nearing death, is able to communicate wordlessly with the hanged workman and draw him back toward life. When he feels her love—which becomes the love and power of God to him—he moans a little, "a moan not quite of pain but of intention and the first faint wellings of recognized obedience and love." But Margaret's love is exchange; she *wills* the death that is coming so that he can be returned to life. That intention of sacrificially relinquishing life becomes part of the greater act; and another, deeper moan answers his, a groan "at once dereliction of power and creation of power. In it, far off, beyond vision in the depths of all the worlds, a god, unamenable to death, awhile endured and died" (*DIH*, pp. 136–37).

Imagery of the cross becomes even more explicit in chapter 7 of *All Hallows' Eve*. Lester is standing, unseen, by Betty's side, helping her to resist the destructive power in Simon's intoning of the reversed Tetragrammaton. But between the two women, one dead and the other about to be sent into the mystery, an exchange of redeeming love has taken place. Lester suddenly feels the conjurations working to destroy *her;* she has become Betty's substitute. At the same time she feels herself supported by a "frame." The love between Betty and Jonathan has worked previously to protect Betty from the oppression of Simon Leclerc. But in this moment only that deeper exchange will avail which involves pardon and substitution.

Lester's atoning act avails also to bring about Father Simon's downfall. Shaken by his failure with Betty, he resorts to cruder magic. But now his magic is twisting upon itself. His house is invaded by a destructive rain, and his magically healed followers begin to revert to their former state of misery. Then Betty enters the magic enclosure and begins further to counter his sorcery. The other images of Simon reappear, and finally all three vanish in a crimson fume. Betty—with power received through Lester, and at the cost of "virtue going out" from her—now brings healing to the inmates of Simon's house. The weird and terrifying appearances of All Hallows' Eve have ceased, the saints have triumphed, and, as dawn glows in the sky, "the Acts of the City" have begun again.

The novels of Charles Williams constitute one great proposition, of which the subject is coinherence. Williams once supplied the predicate for that proposition, as follows: "[Coinherence, actualized by substitution,] is the image everywhere of supernatural charity, and the measure of this or the refusal of this is the cause of all the images."[36] I have examined the novels as an unfolding of various aspects and implications of this controlling idea. They must now be considered as the specifically literary image of the idea.

The reader of a novel by Williams finds himself at the outset confronted by something quite ordinary—a testimonial dinner, a family argument, a walk down a country road, preparations for a play. Where the circumstances are fantastic, they are represented almost as if the situation were an everyday one. This commonplaceness is required by Williams' sacramentalism. The improbabilities are there too, soon enough, but they must break in upon, or emerge from, the more predictable patterns of human life. The story must demonstrate the mutuality of things, the reciprocity of flesh and spirit and of natural and supernatural.

This is accomplished, Williams would insist, by way of images, or symbols. That is, he does not simply construct symbols in order to make a basic idea clearer or more engaging; he discovers things in the actual world of his experience which suggest meanings beyond themselves. "An image exists in its own right, not for the sake of its referent, and not for the sake of the imagist."[37] The power of the human imagination is one such image. Images taken from occult lore are also, as we have seen, important in his fiction. But he came to find his symbolism not so much in the esoteric arts (though he never relinquished this source) as in the actualities of personal relationships and of history in the making.

If all these centers of energy are images, for Williams, of the operation of higher powers and of the power of being as such, then most of the characters in the novels are representatives of various ways of responding to that power: skepticism, cynicism, greed, or reverent submission. The reader is not meant to be concerned primarily with their intrinsic nature; and it is not legitimate, therefore, simply to dismiss Williams' characterization as "flat" or "two-dimensional."

What these novels present us with, however, are not just images of power and images of various responses to such power, but also images of other images. Williams, despite all disclaimers, tends to be an allegorist. Thus the three men in *War in Heaven* who act as

protectors of the Holy Grail—Archdeacon Davenant, the duke of
the North Ridings, and the publisher's clerk Kenneth Mornington
—also represent three other men. Mornington explains it to the
duke:

> "The Archdeacon's Galahad, and you can be Percivale: you're not
> married, are you? And I'm Bors—but I'm not married either and
> Bors was. It doesn't matter; you must be Percivale, because you're a
> poet. And Bors was an ordinary workaday fellow like me. On, on
> to Sarras!" [*WIH,* p. 133].

In turn, the three achievers of the Grail represent, for Williams,
"three degrees of love."[38]

The Place of the Lion is Williams' boldest attempt at bypassing
allegory and creating myth. The explanation of what is going on at
the village of Smetham is to be found—according to the novel—in
a fragmentary, centuries-old treatise by one Marcellus Victorinus
of Bologna, which has been translated by Richardson. The great
Principles of things, the forms of Platonic tradition, are at the same
time the "Angelicals" (the energies of the angelic orders) and the
archetypes of the beasts. Marcellus identifies the first circle as that
of the lion, the second as that of the serpent. The section of the
manuscript which deals with the other orders is missing, except for
the material on the Eagle. But the eagle is of the highest importance,
since only he knows both himself and the others (*POL,* chapter 8).
It becomes clear that the occultist named Foster corresponds to the
lion, his fellow devotee Dora Wilmot to the serpent, Damaris
Tighe's father to the butterfly, Richardson to the unicorn, and
Anthony Durrant to the eagle. The account of Anthony's combat
with Foster and Dora Wilmot makes all this—perhaps too obviously
—evident.

> All round him in the room were noises of hissing and snarling,
> and as he staggered aside in the effort to regain his footing the hot
> breath of one adversary panted into his face, so that it seemed to him
> as if he struggled in the bottom of some loathly pit where foul crea-
> tures fought for their prey. . . . Anthony put all the energy he had
> left into one tremendous outward sweep of his arm, rather as if he
> flung a great wing sideways. . . . In that moment he came to his
> feet, and lightly as some wheeling bird, turned and poised for any
> new attack [*POL,* pp. 92–93].

The meanings are rendered quite explicitly. Berringer, Foster, and Dora Wilmot seek, as human beings will, to know the Principles of things. But they have desired them amiss. Foster wants strength (the lion) without meekness (the lamb); Wilmot, subtlety (the serpent) without wisdom (the phoenix). Both want the powers not out of love for the goodness of being and not with a desire to serve the powers that be, but for their own pride and supremacy. In the flight of the eagle we see the balance which they have disregarded. In Anthony's concern for what is vanishing and in his love for Damaris and Quentin, we find the pattern for proper knowing. "By friendship, by love, these great Virtues [become] delicately known"; otherwise they are seen as their destructive and horrifying counterparts—the eagle a pterodactyl, the rest dinosaurs, behemoths, and other monstrous forms (*POL,* p. 215). *The Place of the Lion* is a parable of creative—and miscreative—knowing, a fictional embodiment of Williams' interpretation of the myth set forth in the first three chapters of Genesis.

The same tendency is seen in the last novels. The images and allusions in *Descent into Hell* associate the action on Battle Hill now with Eden, now with Gomorrah, now with Golgotha, and finally with Zion; the parallels and parodies of *All Hallows' Eve* include Simon as a "trinity" and as "he that should come," Lester on a "cross," Betty performing miraculous cures as "virtue" goes out from her. Williams does not, after all, reveal human universality by creating authentic individuality. Nor, usually, does he surround an image from experience with various hints of meaning in such a way that the story becomes what Richard Eastman has called an "open parable."[39] By way of the more conventional and traditional symbols to which the central images are made to refer, fairly restricted possibilities of meaning are imposed.

This is still not to say, however, that Williams may not be an imagist. For the way of imagery does not necessarily exclude the way of allegory; it may include it as a variant. Williams' writings, Mrs. Shideler asserts, may be

> allegories, written to convey ideas, but the ideas in question were discovered by means of images and are presented in images. The

ascent from image to basis, and the descent from idea to allegorical
symbol, are not mutually exclusive, but complementary.[40]

His is a "corrected" romanticism, in any case, requiring a balance—
even a fusion—of feeling and intellect. It may be that the way of
images corresponds to the exercise of feeling and the development
of allegory to the intellectual component; in that case, the goal will
be a tension between the two ways, a coinherence of image and allegorical symbol. What Williams would be attempting to do, then,
in his novels would be to represent the "romantic experience" with
immediacy and at the same time relate it firmly to a pattern of
thought. All this is consistent with what Williams includes in the
"web of the glory of heaven," or the coinherence: "the recognition
of the good, the exercise of intellect, the importance of interchange,
and [the warrant for allegory] a deliberate relation to the Center."[41]

Where the revelatory experience is connected, fictionally, with
magical things or with poetry, Williams can render that experience
more or less in the manner of a metaphysical ode or lyric, the story
being primarily a "frame" for the impressions of, and reflections on,
the moments of ecstasy. As human relationships become central,
however, he has to find ways of dramatizing these, in action and dialogue, in development of character, in conflict and resolution. He
has also to concern himself with suffering and sin, with the negative
romantic experience and the falsification or betrayal of the true one,
and with redemptive acts of substituted love. The subjects of his
later novels present Williams with new opportunities for a higher
degree of immediacy, richer implications of meaning, and a greater
measure of creative tension. They also confront his art with addi-
tional dangers and difficulties.

Why, given these new concerns, does Williams retain the element
of fantasy? Even in an "exploration of power," the more-than-ordinary power could be a *moral* energy transforming other persons
and the situation in general, but without transgressing the familiar
limits of time and space and the boundary between life and death.
The answer is, of course, that Williams wants precisely the images
of a power that *does* transcend human limitations. The element of
fantasy points to the supernaturalness, just as the commonplace surface suggests the naturalness, in the sacramental reality. Fantasy

also reinforces the idea of the objectivity, the "out-thereness," of grace. Given the fall, Williams would insist,

> any process of redemption would have to operate from within the created world if its integrity were to be preserved. Yet because the co-inherence was riddled with evil, and because the creation could not heal its own wound, redemption would have to come from outside that chaos, deprivation, and antagonism.[42]

Grace is personal, insofar as it operates "from within the created world"; grace is also, however, power, and it must break in from beyond or well up from the undreamed-of depths.

Fantasy is also, for Williams as for C. S. Lewis, part of the "rhetoric" of his fiction. The effect, however, is different. The "romantic experience" on which much of Lewis' fantasy draws is *Sehnsucht,* an intense longing which no object of desire can satisfy and which leads a person to conclude that "the human soul was made to enjoy some object that is never 'fully given.' "[43] For Williams it is the "Beatrician moment" that is decisive. At such a moment one feels that certain things, while remaining what they are, are also more than they seem. It is the power of love that causes this revelation, and the glory which is revealed is itself the coinherence which is "the image everywhere of supernatural charity." Fantasy provides images for the supernatural dimension of the co-inherence and of its refusal; it suggests the possibility that "existence itself is Christian." Williams' fantasy implies an ontology of love.

It could not effectively do so, of course, apart from certain consistencies between theme and narrative technique or style. Ultimately, a Williams novel can be seen to reflect qualities integral to his central theme. The first of these is *inclusiveness.* Considering only the fictional surface, for a moment, we find that in every story except *Descent into Hell* destruction threatens, and salvation preserves, not just a few persons but all mankind. Beneath the surface, at the allegorical level, several of his stories come close to being myths of total explanation; all the great events in salvation-history are included: creation, fall, atonement, judgment, and renovation.

Descent into Hell and *All Hallows' Eve* do not fit this pattern. They must be seen, however, as being very much a part of the overarching mythos of Williams' fiction. The concern in the early

works with origins yields, at the end of Williams' career, to a concern with "last things." Although a good deal is done with the
Eden story in *Descent into Hell,* that novel and *All Hallows' Eve*
are mainly eschatological novels. The ending of Stanhope's play is
the judgment: "Suddenly again, from somewhere in that great abyss
of clarity, a trumpet sounded, and then a great uproar, and then a
single voice. It was the beginning of the end; the judgment of
mortality was there" (*DIH,* p. 208). And so is the ending of the
novel. Stanhope suggests that the various illnesses that have come
upon people like Myrtle Fox and Adela Hunt might be like "one
of the vials of the Apocalypse" (*DIH,* p. 236). For Pauline, however, the painful experiences have been purgatorial. The fire tor-
menting her ancestor is also the flame cleansing her from the stain
of her fear and her incapacity for joy. As the novel ends she thinks
of herself as being in "the easier circles of heaven"(*DIH,* p. 238).

In *All Hallows' Eve* both Lester, newly dead, and Richard, still
in life, embrace the purifying fire. Richard comes to understand that
he must "be born all over again" (*AHE,* p. 215). Lester, her soul
carried by that "merest flicker" of her new friendship with Betty,
finds herself "beginning to live differently" and experiencing "the
beginnings of heaven" (*AHE,* pp. 181, 197). The ending of the
novel is filled with Dantesque images of "the beginnings of heaven."
The multifoliate rose is everywhere. Lester sees a vision of the City,
the life of it "visible as a roseal wonder within" (*AHE,* p. 187).
The approaching dawn of All Saints' Day is anticipated by a "faint
roseal glow." This becomes for Simon "not only a rose-smell but a
smell of blood and of burning, of all those great crimson things"
(*AHE,* p. 265). The rose light thickens around him and his two il-
lusory counterparts, "forming around them, cloud in cloud, overly-
ing like petals" (*AHE,* p. 265) and finally withdraws, carrying him
(or them) away in a fume of crimson, and leaving for the victors
the rosy-fingered dawn of the holy day.

Inclusiveness of scope is felt "spatially" as well as in the linear
dimension. Williams' way of telling a story conveys *universality* of
reference. He does not—as Conrad or Henry James do—restrict
himself to the contents of one consciousness for any length of time,

but moves in and out with great freedom. Even when he is for a time channeling the story through the awareness of a Pauline Anstruther, say, or a Lester Furnival, he provides associations and implications which the subject of the impressions could not be aware of. This is especially the case with Lester and her "cross," the "frame" which supports her as she becomes the sorcerer's substitute victim.

> She pressed herself against the sole support. So those greater than she had come—saints, martyrs, confessors—but they joyously, know-ing that this was the first movement of their re-edification in the City, and that thus in that earliest world fashioned of their earthly fantasies began the raising of the true houses and streets. Neither her mind nor her morals had prepared her for this discovery, nor did she in the least guess what was happening [*AHE*, p. 159].

Lester's limited awareness is made to supply the "natural facts" of coinherence; from his higher vantage point the narrator supplies images and allusions by which to illuminate its supernatural aspect. In his way of telling a story Williams is simply carrying out what he declares to be the obligation of every explorer of the power of being—"to pursue the natural into the more-than-natural of which it is a part."[44]

The style of the novels also betrays the control of a believed pat-tern of ideas. That pattern is influential even upon dialogue. Given Williams' sacramental view of reality and of art, we would expect that conversation would not be mere small talk or, on the other hand, mere exposition of ideas, but would have to be both at once. At times Williams accomplishes this by means of a certain lightness of tone which pervades even discussions of the weightiest matters. Among lovers or friends this may take the form of a knowing inter-change of quotations, allusions, and double meanings. Peter Stan-hope is continually tossing out phrases from the psalms and from Shakespeare. A great deal can be made of casual phrases such as "perfect Babel," or "terribly good," or even "good God." As Richard Furnival—along with Jonathan—forces his way into Betty's room, to take her away from Simon's influence, he says to Lady Walling-ford: "You must forgive this intrusion, Lady Wallingford. We know—Jonathan and I—that we're behaving very badly. But it's absolutely—I do mean *absolutely*—necessary for us to see Betty. If you believe in the Absolute" (*AHE,* pp. 168–69).

The control reaches also to syntax. *Descent into Hell* is a highly schematic novel, with parallels and contrasts set up between Pauline and Adela, Stanhope and Lily Sammile, and even Wentworth and the dead workman. The schematization obtrudes itself particularly with regard to this last parallel, in the balanced sentences of passages such as the following:

> The chamber of that dark fundamental incest had had the dead man for its earliest inhabitant, though his ways and Wentworth's had been far apart—as far as incest from murder, or as self-worship from self-loathing, and either in essence false to all that is. But the self-worship of the one was the potential source of cruelty, as the self-loathing of the other was the actual effect of cruelty; between them lay all the irresolute vacillations of mankind, nourishing the one and producing the other [*DIH,* p. 145].

There are in Williams' novels, as in those of C. S. Lewis, moments of heightening, "eloquent" passages with pretensions to sublimity. In Lewis' fiction such passages are meant to convey something of the ineffable majesty of the "other world." For Williams, the subject of such eloquence is *this* world—but this world glorified, revealed as an immensely complex harmony of flesh and spirit, past and present, natural and supernatural. Strong verbs connote the energy of the love fashioning the great web; convoluted syntax suggests complexity and relationship; allusions, parallels, and imagery delineate the universal pattern into which the particular events and ideas are being woven. Aaron Lee's musings about the mystery of the Fool (in *The Greater Trumps*) evoke many such associations, as well as Williams' most impressive periods:

> But the dark fate that falls on all mystical presentations, perhaps because they are not presentations only, had fallen on this. The doom which struck Osiris in the secular memory of Egypt and hushed the holy, sweet, and terrible Tetragrammaton in the ritual of Judah, and wounded the Keeper of the Grail in the Castle of the Grail, and by the hand of the blind Hoder pierced the loveliest of all the Northern gods, and after all those still everywhere smote and divided and wounded and overthrew and destroyed by the sin of man and yet by

more and other than the sin of man, for the myth of gods and rebellious angels had been invoked—by reason, no doubt, to explain, but by something deeper than reason to frame the sense of a dreadful necessity in things: the need that was and yet must not be allowed to be, the inevitability that must be denied, the fate that must be rejected, so only and only by such contradictions of mortal thought did the nature of the universe make itself felt by man [*GT,* pp. 177–78].

In such passages a third characteristic of Williams' method and style is disclosed—namely, the illusion of *simultaneity.* For one thing, Williams is not so much concerned in his novels in creating authentic persons and arousing the reader's interest in a sequence of changes which they undergo as he is in representing certain responses to situations and events and making the reader aware of a pattern of such responses built around a central situation. What Williams said of Blake's literary preferences is true of his own fiction also: "He is interested . . . in states of being, rather than individuals."[45]

In the end Williams develops his own variety of "spatial form," sequential time becoming less and less a determinative element as he seeks to trace the timeless pattern of the glory. In each of the last two novels, particularly, there is one moment, coming not far after the midpoint of the action, which seems almost to bring time to a stop. What is done in that moment affects several persons decisively, and it also participates in the cosmic act of atonement; the moment is—in a double meaning that Williams would have enjoyed—crucial. In *Descent into Hell* it is the moan of the dead workman, signifying for him the beginning of repentance and restoration, for Margaret Anstruther the acceptance of death, for Wentworth the seal of damnation, and for mankind the "dereliction of power and creation of power" enacted upon the cross. In *All Hallows' Eve* it is Betty's whispering "Lester"—which counters the magical incantation and thus preserves Betty, brings a new sense of trust to Lester, communicates a life-changing glimpse of glory to Richard, and marks the beginning of the end for Simon.

The intricate, allusive, evocative passages I have already described also contribute to the illusion of timelessness. In this respect the style of such passages partakes of the nature of ritual. Its allusions to mythical events are a way of repeating the primordial and thus evoking the eternal. The incantatory power of its rhythms, furthermore, is a technique for transcending individual self-consciousness and thus genuinely celebrating the power of being as such. Here Charles Williams is like Milton, and his comments on "ceremony" in Miltonic verse have a double application.

> One of the advantages of ceremony, rightly used, is that it gives a place to self-consciousness, and a means whereby self-consciousness may be lost in the consciousness of the office filled or the ritual carried out. The art of Milton's poetry is its self-consciousness absorbed in ceremony.[46]

Such a timeless, selfless contemplation of the eternal constitutes *vision*. Now, it would appear that Williams repudiates the notion that vision is something higher than faith. The stand taken by the church against the Gnostics would seem to have been his position also. "*See, understand, enjoy,* said the Gnostic; *repent, believe, love,* said the Church, *and if you see anything by the way, say so.*"[47] But it is also true that he speaks of three levels of faith: "I believe Christ, I believe in Christ, within Christ I believe. The progress is from formal belief to real belief, and then to unitive belief."[48] The highest power of love is that in which one has the sense of loving from the great web itself, of living *within* the beloved. And the third mode or level of coinherence distinguished by Williams is the vision of universal coinherence.

The greatest literature too seems to be, for him, the literature of vision. In its last phase, "the beatitude of poetry," the mind of Shakespeare finds itself "capable of imagining essential fact and almost of non-human existence."[49] All poetry, Anthony Durrant comes to realize, is "the approach of the fallen understanding to that unfallen meaning" (*POL,* p. 218). The ending of Stanhope's play brings Pauline a similar illumination: "From the edge of eternity the poets were speaking to the world, and two modes of experience were mingled in that sole utterance" (*DIH,* pp. 208-9). Williams' novels are not *about* the vision; they want to *be* the vision. Vision is not granted to the main characters in a Williams novel, although sometimes a secondary character such as Margaret Anstruther is given special insight. Pauline and Lester remain at the second level of coinherence, that of the *experience* of substituted love in human relationships. The vision that apprehends everything in a moment of ecstatic knowing is not for the creature within this fictional world but for its creator, and for the reader. Professor Cormican says, with reference to *Paradise Lost:* "The reader is expected to survey the actions of Satan, Adam, and Eve from the calm beatitude of Heaven, that is, with as close an approximation to God's own view as human nature, elevated by grace, permits."[50] This is useful advice for the reader of Charles Williams also. For in his novels the concern for the integrity of the human images of love ultimately yields to the desire for the unobstructed vision of the Love which moves the sun and the other stars.

I have said that the fiction of Charles Williams can be called (to use the phrase with which he described the poetry of his own Peter Stanhope) "the powerful exploration of power after his own manner." I have attempted to chart that exploration, setting forth the interrelated themes of the novels, and to analyze the qualities of "his own manner," the characteristic structure, technique, and style. There remains only to question the justness of the adjective "powerful." The question to be asked is this: Since there is clearly a correlation between Williams' way of writing a novel and his way of looking at the world, can a similar correlation be discovered between the strengths and weaknesses of those novels and the particular emphases within that pattern of belief?

The "ordinariness" of situations and persons which I have remarked in Williams' fiction is characteristic of many works of fantasy. There, however, it often merely enhances the shock at the discovery of or invasion by the unknown powers. In his novels these elements are images of the indispensable presence of the natural within the sacramental reality. Williams thus seems to place himself in the tradition of Irenaeus, say, rather than in the more ascetic tradition of St. Thomas. For Aquinas, the sacraments seem to be "God's gracious concession to man's regrettably sensuous nature"; for Irenaeus and the "classical" view they are symbols of the ultimate unity of nature and grace. Redemption is not escape from the evils of the present environment, but the restoration of "health" and the development of maturity. Even now, when our redemption is not complete, there remains a residual goodness and health throughout the whole life of the physical universe, because of the immanence of the eternal Word.[51] In both his fictional and his theological writings this would seem to be Williams' view of the human, natural, and physical in relation to the divine, supernatural, and spiritual.

There is in Williams, however, another line of thought about the body, about our natural state. Lester Furnival, "embodied"—along with Evelyn—in the dwarf woman shaped by Simon's magic, begins to see this hideous form as an image of the human body in its fallen condition. She knows her body in life to have been no more than "this false deformed death" unless—the thought comes to her— "unless she could still let it be what it had been ordained to be, worthy in its whole physical glory of Betty, of Richard, of the City she felt about her, of all that was unfamiliar to her in the name of God" (*AHE,* p. 232). In theological works Williams speculates occasionally concerning the body of the "unfallen" Adam. Before the fall perhaps man possessed a special consciousness, of simultaneity as well as temporality. His whole fundamental mode of existence was divine. Rejecting the Creator, man "rejected also the natural life. . . . Our physical nature was dragged down with our spiritual and labored, as it labors still, in a state it was never meant to endure."[52]

The quasi-Gnostic attitude toward nature finds only a small place, if any place at all, in Williams' thought. It is obvious, however, that the image of the natural—the "ordinariness" I have described— suffers in the novels at the expense of the fantastic, the image of the supernatural. This can be detected first of all, perhaps, in a certain banality in much of the dialogue, particularly where one feels that the dialogue is there simply to "fill in" between fantastic happenings.

Williams falls into a comparable "thinness" in characterization. Again, this is not to say that the so-called "flat" or "two-dimensional" character is to be despised. As Edwin Muir has argued, against critics like E. M. Forster: "The question is for what sufficient reason both kinds, the flat and the round, should exist."[53] In Williams' first three novels flat characters are entirely adequate for what the novels intend. All three might be called novels of perception. An occult energy makes itself felt and elicits various responses. Gradually the people who matter in the story come to understand the capabilities of this force, the nature of the struggle which its appearance has precipitated, and the response which will best serve the greater power it represents. The action is melodramatic, conflict is external, and except for the arrival at perception there is little change in the persons involved. The later novels, however, come closer to being novels of redemption. The supernatural power may still be associated with magical objects and the sorcerer's arts, but it is more importantly manifested in human relationships of friendship and love. But this development entails conflict, suffering, pardon, transformation. The last four novels arouse new expectations but by and large fall short of fulfilling them. In *Descent into Hell* Pauline's struggle actually comes to an end easily and early, through the power of Peter Stanhope's exhortations; all that remains is, so to speak, to enact the ceremony. The sin which has to be repented of and pardoned in *All Hallows' Eve* is never represented; it is all in the past and must simply be talked about. As for pardon and substitution, one confrontation—that between Lester and Betty—has pretty much to do for all. What happens in these books is that whatever concern is aroused with respect to everyday human conflict arising out of fear or love or pride is at once swept away to give place to the excitement of fantastic happenings. Again Williams is following the natural into the more-than-natural of which it is a part.

I am not concerned, at this point, to argue for or against supernaturalism, as such. The question is what Williams' supernaturalism may or may not mean to the climate of his fictional world. Such a view in general would hold, of course, that man's life is the product of creaturely processes and is lived out in the world of space and time, but that the ultimate foundation and final destiny of man lie in a supratemporal relation to the reality which transcends all creaturely existence.[54] What tends to be lost in Williams' fiction is the two-sidedness; he is too eager—given the expectations which his later novels arouse in the reader—to move beyond "creaturely processes" and the "world of space and time" into the transcendent and the supratemporal.

This is not to deny, however, the power of the novels at many points to convey a sense of the interpenetration of the two realms. The degree of that power is in proportion, I believe, to the seriousness with which Williams takes the claims of both aspects of his reality. T. S. Eliot insists, in the introduction which he wrote for *All Hallows' Eve,* that for Williams "there was no frontier between the material and the spiritual world" (*AHE,* p. xiii). For James Agee, too, it was this quality which made Williams—as Agee put it—"one of the very few contemporary writers who moves and interests me to read." With *Descent into Hell* particularly in mind, he speaks of Williams' "wonderful gift for conveying, and dramatizing, the 'borderline' states of mind or Being."[55]

I find this even more true—especially of the beginning—of *All Hallows' Eve.* We are given no immediate indication of what Lester's true state is. Gradually she learns, and we with her—through the strange silence, the absence of people, the absurd length of this "lull," the appearance (followed by the fading away) of her husband, Richard—that she is dead, having been killed by the plane that crashed on her and her friend Evelyn. The even more subtle things that are going on in this opening chapter can only be suggested by quoting at some length. In the first paragraph, for instance, there is both an ironic suggestion of Wordsworth's famous sonnet and a pervasive sense of a double meaning—one for the people of the City and one for Lester—in the references to the peace which is not yet a "formal peace" and to the "boredom and suffering and misery" which the future still holds.

> She was standing on Westminster Bridge. It was twilight, but the City was no longer dark. The street lamps along the Embankment were still dimmed, but in the buildings shutters and blinds and curtains had been removed or left undrawn, and the lights were coming out there like the first faint stars above. Those lights were the peace. It was true that formal peace was not yet in being; all that had happened was that the fighting had ceased. The enemy, as enemy, no longer existed and one more crisis of agony was done. Labor, intelligence, patience—much need for these; and much certainty of boredom and suffering and misery, but no longer the sick vigils and daily despair.

The simplicity and at the same time the richness of implication of a passage such as this remind us that the way of Charles Williams is intended to be the way of images. The image is to be not so much the illustration for a believed idea as the key to the unknown. In Williams' novels it is easy to see how the human imagination and how human relationships could be taken as images, both participating in the power of being. It is easy to "believe in" these images as keys to the unknown. What is more difficult is the question as to whether or not his interest in the occult also provides him with that sense of actuality combined with import out of which images grow. If it does—and I have already suggested that Williams does take occultism seriously—then it would seem that he could make up for his relative failure to present convincing images of human relationships by concentrating on constructing images out of fantasy so as to evoke convincingly the experience of the supernatural. Fantasy based on occult lore could provide effective images at least of the undifferentiated and unreflective experience of the divine power and presence.

But just as "realistic" characterization and dialogue are slighted so that fantasy can be exploited, so the power of fantasy to suggest "Otherness" yields to its usefulness for explaining and arguing a highly articulated pattern of beliefs about the Christian God. This allegorical thrust, I have said, reveals itself in the "doubleness" of the story being told, the intrusive techniques of narration, and the allusive eloquence of certain pivotal passages. In *Descent into Hell,* when Peter Stanhope has been explaining the doctrine of substituted love to Pauline, he adds: "There's no need to introduce Christ, unless you wish. It's a fact of experience" (*DIH,* p. 106). But Charles Williams introduces him, when the moan of the dead workman outside Margaret Anstruther's window on Battle Hill merges into a groan which shakes the mountain. "The groan was at once dereliction of power and creation of power. In it, far off, beyond vision in the depths of all the worlds, a god, unamenable to death, awhile endured and died" (*DIH,* p. 137).

Descent into Hell contains, in the account of Wentworth's damnation, the highest achievement of Williams' imagination. His descent is measured by ordinary—almost trivial—acts which are realistically presented: his petulance at the knighting of Aston Moffatt, his jealousy of Adela, his refusal even to go to the trouble of telling the truth about the authenticity of the costumes for Stanhope's play. Yet the changes taking place within him are also objectified in elements of fantasy—the "false Adela," the dream of descending the rope, and his loss of contact with the world around him at the end of the novel. But even here—where Williams succeeds so admirably with both images drawn from ordinary experience and those partaking of the nature of fantasy—the Idea ungracefully intrudes. The reenactment of the Eden myth by Wentworth is too lengthy and too labored; and it contains one wretched attempt at something Williams never quite succeeded in bringing off, the random associations of interior monologue:

> It was good for him to be here, and great fun; one day he would laugh, but laughter would be tiring here, under trees and leaves, leaves—leaves and eaves—eaves and eves; a word with two meanings, and again a word with two meanings, eves and Eves. Many Eves to many Adams; one Eve to one Adam; one Eve to each, one Eve to all. Eve . . . [*DIH*, p. 91].

I have said much about the incarnational bent of Williams' thinking. The particular form it takes, however, is indicated by his many references to the clause in the so-called Athanasian Creed which specifies that the incarnation is "not by conversion of the Godhead into flesh but by taking of the manhood into God." In *The Descent of the Dove,* Williams reads this clause as a vindication of the human and the natural. "It is the actual manhood which is to be carried on, and not the height which is to be brought down. All images are, in their degree, to be carried on; mind is never to put off matter; all experience is to be gathered in."[56] Carried over into literature, this formula means that the God-bearing image does not confer revelation, so to speak, from above, but "raises the beholder to the vision of God in a movement from nature to that which is above and beyond nature."[57] The images of Williams' novels—fantastic and otherwise —are made the vehicles for the truth about God and his dealings with men. But what is "above" inevitably encroaches upon the power of what is "below." There is hierarchy rather than reciprocity. Like C. S. Lewis, Williams inclines to the Alexandrine view of the

incarnation—"this person is God living and acting humanly"—
rather than the Antiochene—"this person is the Man in whom God
lives and acts." He is unwilling to affirm a real "reciprocal relationship" which arises out of, though it is not exhausted in, "the loving
inclination of divine and human selves towards each other."[58]

According to a number of statements in his literary criticism, what
Williams expects to discover in the highest literary art is the mainte-
nance of tension between image and idea and between real and
ideal. Williams' criterion for high achievement in poetry is the
presence of the "feeling intellect." Yet in the novels, as we have seen,
the intellect often seems to take control, so that what is produced is
the *pattern* of the glory. If Docetism involves relaxing the hold on
the reality of the image in itself in order to examine that to which
the image refers, Charles Williams may well be suspected of the
literary manifestation of this ancient deviation.[59]

Not only are the "ordinary" elements swallowed up by fantasy,
and the fantasy in turn patterned into allegory; the allegory itself is
under the control of certain dogmatic presuppositions which further
influence the structure and style of Williams' fiction. His respect for
"the epigram of experience which is in all dogma" (*DIH*, p. 210) is,
of course, simply an aspect of that "deliberate relation to the Center"
which he finds to be one of the patterns in the "web." And, for all
his talk about the indeterminacy of the image, Williams is not able
to say that one derives from experience alone whatever can be said
about the Creator of that experience. His theology begins with the
teaching church and the authoritative creeds; his fiction is not discovery but rather the communication of received truth.

The ontology which is presupposed in Williams' fiction is partly
inherent in the dogmatic formulations to which he subscribes and
partly derived from his particular reading of them. With his typically
Anglican incarnational bias, for example, Williams is closer at certain points to the tradition of the Greek fathers than to that of the
Latins. Whereas the Latin fathers stressed a moral duality of sin and
healing grace, the Greeks stressed an ontological duality of nature
and *supernatural* grace.[60] But one of the dangers of such an approach
—whether from the influence of Platonic thought or from intensity
of devotion—is monism. Williams (in radical contrast with C. S.

Lewis) is attracted by monism. For the great truth he teaches is that existence is good and must be known as good. Worked out consistently, such a view makes it difficult to deal adequately with evil and suffering and even to do full justice to the reality of human sinfulness.

In theory Williams is cognizant of the power of darkness. C. S. Lewis insists that Charles Williams contained within himself a skeptic, even a pessimist. He felt the pain of life in the world. His conversation was not gloomy in tone, but he said dark things. He insisted that God approves of the frightened, voluble creature called Job.[61] The early novels present skeptics sympathetically, and several of his plays emphasize the terror associated with the love of God. His essay "The Cross" goes deepest into this sense of "outrage." It is not tolerable, Williams asserts, that for men "a finite choice ought to result in an infinite distress." Therefore there is a need to "justify the act of creation."

> The Cross justifies it to this extent at least—that just as he submitted us to His inexorable will, so he submitted Himself to our wills (and therefore to His). . . . He deigned to endure the justice He decreed.[62]

There is much to suggest, then, that Williams takes evil seriously and places a high valuation on what he calls, in *The Descent of the Dove*, the "quality of disbelief."

The novels, however, weaken this impression. The skeptics of the early stories are quickly convinced, or at least silenced. The evil forces are always utterly routed. Temptation and sin do not reach deeply into the lives of Pauline or Lester. They are ready for conversion; all that is needed is a moral teacher such as Stanhope or an opportunity for self-examination such as Lester receives. Love is the theme, I have said, of all Williams' fiction; yet in *The Place of the Lion, The Greater Trumps,* and *All Hallows' Eve* there is little genuine opposition for love to overcome. The exception to all this is Lawrence Wentworth in *Descent into Hell.* It is ironic and perhaps significant that Williams, who stresses in all his work the goodness of creation, should achieve his greatest success depicting a character who stubbornly insists, to the very end, on knowing good as evil.

Williams' ontological presuppositions incline him also toward

timeless structure rather than toward rhythmic process. His metaphors for his favorite concept of coinherence include words like
"web" and "diagram," as well as "pattern." This tendency helps to
produce in the novels a strong sense of the interrelatedness of things.
But the representation of the human experience of time becomes
problematical. What R. R. Niebuhr says about the theological notion
of *Heilsgeschichte* can be applied with justice to Williams' novels,
particularly the last two: there is no movement except that "as it
expounds the ultimate meaning of a hypothetical totality of experience, there is a progression from the postulated premises to the
elicited conclusion."[63] The possibility of exchange and substitution
as an act overleaping the limitations of time and even the boundary
of death is an idea with great power. It generates the images of
fantasy in *Descent into Hell* and *All Hallows' Eve*, and these books
represent Williams' powers at their best. But this concept carries a
price; it requires a view of time that tends to make movement and
change unreal. Eternity, for Williams, is always the *nunc stans*; "in
the place of the Omnipotence there is neither before nor after; there
is only act" (*DIH*, p. 110). Time, he seems to say, following Kant,
is simply a form of man's perception. But this can produce the kind
of thinking which becomes explicit in some of his remarks about the
cross. Our faith, Williams says, is a trust in what is already done.
"Not only His act," he goes on, "but all our acts are finished so. . . .
It is finished; we too do but play out the necessary ceremony."[64]
Williams seems almost to exclude time from sacramental interchange.

If time is unreal, then so is freedom. To say, as Williams seems to
do, that willed necessity is freedom, willed hierarchy equality, and
to dismiss our actions in life as simply the playing out of the necessary ceremony, is to consign man to an essentially passive role. It is
worth recalling how many of the persons in Williams' novels are
simply "paths" for the irruptive power. Williams clearly wants to
say that grace operates both from within creation and from "outside." But the overemphasis on fantasy at the expense of the everyday, the dominance of allegorical idea over image, the lack of conflict and suffering, the decreasing importance of sequential time—
all these tendencies make the divine action so preeminent, the power

D

of grace so overriding, the opposition so futile that all seems over at the beginning and reading the novel, too, is simply seeing the necessary ceremony played out before us. *All Hallows' Eve* strengthens this impression through an emphasis on the objective efficacy (ex opere operato) of the sacraments which recalls to mind Graham Greene's novel *The End of the Affair*. In Williams' story, as in Greene's, the sacrament in question is baptism, and the difficulty is that someone is supernaturally influenced as an adult by virtue of a baptism which she has no idea ever took place. The last point is not quite true of Betty Wallingford, in *All Hallows' Eve*, for she dimly remembers being put down into and lifted out of the water of a small lake and hearing a woman (her nurse) say: "There, dearie, no one can undo that; bless God for it" (*AHE*, pp. 134–35). But, it finally becomes evident, "this child of magic [has] been saved from magic by a mystery beyond magic" (*AHE*, p. 208). The rain which, at the end, beats in upon Simon in his own house, contributing to his downfall, is also carefully connected with the baptism. Even Jonathan and Richard shrink from that rain. But Betty, we are told, "still fresh from the lake of power, the wise waters of creation, lifted her face to it and felt it nourishing her" (*AHE*, pp. 266–67).

Taken as a whole the novels of Charles Williams present an impressive—at times a magnificent—vision of the universe itself as Love, as a vast coinherence which is "the image everywhere of supernatural charity." One can feel only admiration for the attempt to give love an ontological base, rather than treating it merely as a human emotion. It is gratifying, too, to find in Williams, as in Paul Tillich, a genuine concern to work out the relationships among the varieties of love, rather than collapse the tension in favor of something like Anders Nygren's extreme exaltation of the self-giving element. But these facts cannot be allowed to conceal another significant fact—namely, that here in Williams' fiction is a conception of love in which the elements of individuality and freedom are clearly given less than their due.

The tradition to which Williams is so deeply indebted has bequeathed to him another problem with regard to the understanding of love. As Gilson reminds us, within this tradition particular goods are taken to be analogues of the creative Good. If one loves the image, this means also that he loves the original. However, if he knows it to be an image, he will, of course, prefer the original.[65] But the highest faculty in "human nature" is the rational faculty, and the highest goal is the intellectual vision of what is highest. Since this best part of man, reason, is able to transcend the here and now—so as to know "absolutely" and, in a sense, "timelessly"—man's desire must be for what is eternal.[66] The question, then, is how to love a particular creaturely existent, concretely and for itself—to love the actual, living human being (Berdyaev says) as well as the divine image in him, to love man in God as well as God in man.[67] If what is most important in me is the activity of knowing which is directed toward the general in the particular, toward the formal, measurable, and comparable in all occasions, then my existence is first of all in the presence of ideas or patterns or universals. I am in relation, of course, to other beings; but any such relationship, including that of love, is a function of my relation to the objects of reason.[68]

Vision is finally determinative for Williams' understanding of love. Sin is knowing the good as evil; redemption is a reorientation of knowledge; the glory for man is the ultimate vision. In a Williams novel, a power makes itself felt, the power of grace which also contains the terror that is inseparable from the good; a man is shaken out of (or confirms himself in) his self-centered immediacy and is directed into a true knowledge of the total coinherent pattern of things (or consigned to the damnation he has instead chosen). Given the novel on the terms implied within its structure and its themes, what we ask of Williams is the assurance that this power addresses itself to man's self-determination, that time is taken seriously in the working out of his salvation or his damnation, and that the delight in the particularity of things and their independent existence has not been relinquished in favor of the lonely, transcendent vision.

Yet on the question of time it has been argued—and rightly, I believe—that Williams "tends to confer on the Beatrician moment in its first manifestation a total redemptive power immediately operative."[69] There is little of what might be called "growing into" the coinherence. Structurally this tendency takes the form of a ritualistic and iconic treatment of symbols. Williams names a thing briefly, then later implicitly indicates that the name is meant to stand for some larger conception. He uses his symbols as icons, as reminders of truths already believed in. "In iconography the final justification rests not in the image but in the system of which it is a part."[70] But the contract that Williams makes with us in his novels grants us the right to expect the maintaining of a certain tension, a genuine coinherence, within such pairs of concepts as the natural and the supernatural, the image and the idea, the existential and the ontological, evil and good, freedom and necessity, temporality and eternity, human love and heavenly vision. Where the tension is seriously weakened, we can only conclude that Charles Williams must be (in John Bayley's phrase) "in love with his own vision and with his characters as projections of it."[71]

The novels of Charles Williams raise in us higher hopes than do those of C. S. Lewis, but they disappoint us more. Through the interplay of everyday situations and fantastic events he begins to convey the mysterious depths of meaning which can be discovered beneath the most commonplace action or response; then he allows his ever-complicating devices of fantasy to overwhelm the reader's attention and virtually do away with the two-sidedness he originally led the reader to anticipate. Next, the power of the fantasy claims attention in its own right, a welter of images suggesting that "there are more things in heaven and earth" than are dreamt of in our philosophy—until he turns to using his gift for fantasy as a means for imposing on us his own philosophy. Despite the imposition we find that his images, even bound as they are to the pattern of ideas which constitutes received truth for Williams, begin to impress us with the possibility that existence itself may be Christian, that wherever there is an act of true humanity there is Christ, that every act of forgiveness is the cross, and that we can confront the nothingness in life because in so doing we encounter the Christ who has gone before us into the darkness; then, however, he lifts it beyond our grasp by incorporating all these things in a supratemporal, suprapersonal vision of the whole. About to demonstrate the proposition that the power of being itself is the energy of Love, he instead projects a vision of power such as to inhibit the freedom, temporality, and concrete individuality without which love is merely empty form.

J. R. R. TOLKIEN: FANTASY AND THE PHENOMENOLOGY OF HOPE

CHAPTER 3

For J. R. R. Tolkien, fantasy is the art of creating an "other world." It is an "elvish craft," and the "secondary world" thus produced is a realm of enchantment.[1] As a multitude of readers can now testify, to enter the "other world" called Middle-earth is to encounter both the strange and the familiar and, emanating from them, an extraordinary power.

To one reading *The Lord of the Rings*[2] for the first time, that power may be felt simply as a *sense* of depths, of rich implications. But depth and richness, considered analytically, become levels or dimensions; I shall try to suggest the three dimensions of *The Lord of the Rings*. On reading Tolkien's work we find ourselves first in a dimension of *wonder,* the effect of authentic fantasy. On further reading we sense also a dimension of *import* or meaningfulness, the allegorical thrust of the fantasy. Finally, we may discover a dimension of incipient *belief,* a function of the "rhetoric" of this fiction, of what I have dared to call its "strategy."

First, then, the appeal of *The Lord of the Rings* lies in the fact that it *is*—so wholeheartedly and unabashedly—fantasy. This is the realm of Faërie, where dwell elves, fays, witches, trolls, and dragons; where sky and sea, tree and stone, bird and beast can all be changed by magical enchantment; and where men, too, can see strange sights and be made capable of more-than-human deeds. The literary expression of what is conceived by the fantastic imagination carries a quality of strangeness and wonder. It evokes in the reader an equivalent sense of wonder and a longing for this other mode of life. In fact, Tolkien insists, such fantasy contributes to the satisfaction of certain primordial human desires, and to be successful it need not convince the reader of the possibility, but only of the desirability, of the Secondary World.[3]

Whether or not Tolkien is correct in granting fantasy such universal powers, his conviction about it stands him in good stead. It inspires him to invent not a "thin," sketchy other world as a mere frame for allegory but a rich, substantial world. It carries him so far, indeed, that to the one-thousand-plus pages of narrative he appends over one hundred pages of miscellaneous information about Middle-earth. It also gives him the boldness to plunge us directly and totally into the fantasy realm, rather than to take us there from the earth we know by space ship or time machine or to bring the powers of another, occult world into everyday human life.

Something must be said, first, about the *geography* of this other world. The events of the story take place at a time and in a place which are for us indeterminate but which are identified in the book as the Third Age of Middle-earth—more exactly, the western part of the great landmass known as Middle-earth. To the west and south-west is the Sea. What lies far to the east we are not told. As for the climate, the range seems to be pretty much that of our Europe. Accordingly, with some exceptions the animals and birds found in the forests are those which we know today.

But this does not begin to say all that needs to be said. In Middle-earth a forest can be a special sort of menace. As Frodo and his companions make their way through the Old Forest they find that the trees, not liking strangers, are moving so as to head them off and lead them where they do not wish to go. After a time, through the heaviness of the air and the whispered song of its boughs, an old willow puts them all to sleep, then imprisons two of them in a crack and tries to drown a third. Mountains too can be dangerous. The Fellowship of the Ring, on their way south, try to cross the Misty Mountains by way of Mount Caradhras, only to find their lives imperiled by a sudden snowstorm and rockslide which they can only attribute to the malevolence of Caradhras the Cruel.

Both trees and water are transfigured in Lothlórien, where Elves still dwell. Winter flowers bloom in unfading grass, and in autumn the leaves of the trees do not fall but turn to gold and remain until the new green opens in the spring. Frodo lays his hand upon one of these trees and knows suddenly, more keenly than ever before, "the feel and texture of a tree's skin and of the life within it . . . the delight of the living tree itself" (1. 366).

Everything in this fantasy world is thus capable of being more "alive," more "personal" than its counterpart in our everyday world. Birds and animals can be good, like the eagle Gwaihir the Windlord, or evil, like the birds that act as spies for the evil Sauron. It is a supernatural darkness that rolls out of Mordor to cover Gondor during the siege, and things in Lórien radiate a more-than-ordinary luminousness. Evil creatures can be driven back by the fiery light of the wizard Gandalf's staff. Certain strong and wise persons are able to use the *palantírs,* the Seeing-stones of Númenor, to see far off and to converse in thought with others who possess such stones. There is food, such as the *lembas* of Lórien, and drink, such as the *miruvor* of Rivendell, which have special efficacy to revive those who partake of them.

In such a fairy-tale world, actions beyond "nature" are taken for granted. The possibility of such supernatural action is conceived of because of the form of our active existence. We are aware of ourselves as active beings in interaction with an environment of other agents. We can vary the form or intensity of our activities; in other words, within our nature we are free. But that sense of freedom leads us to dream of passing through to supernatural deeds. When we attribute such action to trees and mountains and to more-than-human creatures, we have created the realm of faërie.[4]

A number of the creatures living in the environment I have just characterized are also other than ordinary. An *ethnography* of Middle-earth should begin, I think, with the Elves. In places like Mirkwood or Lothlórien one sees the fair, tall forms of Elves and hears their lovely singing. They came from, and they return to, the Blessed Realm beyond the farthest seas. Because they live in both worlds at once, they possess special powers. They are valiant, too, against evil, but primarily so as to preserve good things from the past rather than to create new conditions. But, as Men multiply, the time of the Elves is drawing to a close. Few of the Grey-elven and even fewer of the Eldar, or Elven-wise, are to be found in Middle-earth. Although there is no evil in their dwelling places, they suffer the effects of evil. They cannot die, however, but, instead, leave their dwellings in Mirkwood or Lórien or Rivendell and make their way westward to the Havens, where Círdan the Shipwright still abides, and from there set sail for the Undying Realm.

A few even more ancient inhabitants survive, such as the Ents, the giant shepherds of the trees. Treebeard, the guardian of Fangorn, is "the oldest living thing that still walks beneath the Sun upon this Middle-earth" (2. 102). He is "a large Man-like, almost Troll-like, figure, at least fourteen feet high, very sturdy, with a tall head and hardly any neck," covered with something like green or gray bark. "The large feet had seven toes each," the description continues. "The lower part of the long face was covered with a sweeping grey beard, bushy, almost twiggy at the roots, thin and mossy at the ends." His voice is like a deep woodwind instrument, and his eyes, brown, shot with a green light, seem to lead into "an enormous well behind them, filled up with ages of memory and long, slow, steady thinking" (2. 66).

Another fairly numerous race in Middle-earth is that of the Dwarves. They are a tough, secretive, laborious people, lovers of "things that take shape under the hands of the craftsmen rather than of things that live by their own life" (and thus are different from, and antagonistic toward, the Elves [3. 410]). They live mostly underground and mainly in the north, under the Lonely Mountain in Erebor or in the Iron Hills east of there. Once they lived in great numbers in the mountains far to the west and also delved deep in the Mines of Moria under the Misty Mountains. They are short, usually bearded, rough-and-ready in manner. They speak the languages of Men, but have a secret language of their own, heard briefly in Gimli's battle cry at Helm's Deep: *Baruk Khazâd! Khazâd ai-mênu!*

Orcs and Trolls are the evil instruments of the Dark Power. Bred by the Dark Power in the Elder Days, the Orcs are the counterfeits of Elves, just as Trolls are the counterfeits of Ents (2. 89). Orcs are found in Mordor, Sauron's realm in the southeast and with the wizard Saruman in Isengard, and a few still linger in the far north and the Misty Mountains. As to their appearance, Tolkien gives few details: a suggestion of a generally manlike structure, with such animal characteristics as long arms, fangs, clawlike hands. They are coarse, spiteful, quarrelsome, greedy, sadistic. They speak a debased form of the Common Speech, as well as the Black Speech which Sauron has imposed upon them, a language which sounds like this: *Ugluk u bagronk sha pushdug Saruman-glob búbhosh skai.*

Over against the ancient Treebeard, who is good or at least neutral, Middle-earth also disgorges its evil creatures from earliest days. The chronicles of the Dwarves tell of a time in the middle of the Third Age when, delving for *mithril* in Khazad-dûm (Moria), they "roused from sleep a thing of terror that . . . had lain hidden at the foundations of the earth since the coming of the Host of the West: a Balrog of Morgoth" (3. 352). In describing the Balrog, Tolkien gives only what the horrified members of the Fellowship see, and that consists merely of a confused impression of its huge and fiery presence and of the power and terror that seemed to go before it. In a tunnel near the Tower of Cirith Ungol at the west entrance to Mordor lurks another monster, the noisome Shelob:

> There agelong she had dwelt, an evil thing in spider-form . . . and she served none but herself, drinking the blood of Elves and Men, bloated and grown fat with endless brooding on her feasts, weaving webs of shadow; for all living things were her food, and her vomit darkness [2. 332].

But the specific antagonists of the Nine Walkers of the Fellowship of the Ring are the Nine Riders, the Ringwraiths. These were Men of Númenor who had fallen into dark wickedness; the Enemy gave them the nine rings of power and devoured them, so that they became living ghosts, or wraiths. Faceless and formless, they wear their black robes only to give shape to their nothingness. In the first part of the story they ride upon horses, as the Black Riders; later, as the Nazgûl, upon huge winged creatures. Their leader is the long-ago witch-king of Angmar, who—so the prophecy runs—can never be destroyed by man (3. 92). Their very flight overhead brings despair, their poisoned wounds cause slow, cold death.

These are only servants of the central embodiment of evil, Sauron, the Dark Lord of the Rings. Once his seat of power was at Dol Guldur in Mirkwood. Driven from there he made his way south to desolate, mountain-walled Mordor. There, in the tower of Barad-dûr, he plans and controls almost all that is evil. He is symbolized as the great red searching Eye.

An appendix tells us that when perhaps a thousand years had passed in the Third Age, the Wizards appeared in Middle-earth, "messengers sent to contest the power of Sauron and to unite all those who had the will to resist him" (3. 365). They came in the shape of Men, but they have aged only very slowly and possess great powers. Saruman the White is the greatest of his order, having, in addition to the usual powers, an irresistible, spellbinding voice. He has also the greatest knowledge of the arts of the Enemy. But those long years of study have brought him under the influence of Sauron, and he has changed. Gandalf the Grey (called Mithrandir by the Elves) is the wizard who has both power and goodness. He is, as Faramir of Gondor says, "a great mover of the deeds that are done in our time" (2. 279).

The Men of this region of Middle-earth—as Faramir also tells Frodo and Sam—can be classified as "the High, or Men of the West, which were Númenoreans; and the Middle Peoples, Men of the Twilight, such as are the Rohirrim and their kin that dwell still far in the North; and the Wild, the Men of Darkness" (2. 287). Most of the descendants of the Númenoreans now live in Gondor in the south, the center of which is the great stone city of Minas Tirith. But they have mingled their blood with that of lesser men and are now a failing people, with memories and tokens of their heroic past. The Rohirrim, the Masters of Horses from Rohan—also called the Eorlings or the Men of the Riddermark—are allies of Gondor. They speak a language of their own, which Tolkien "translates" so as to suggest Old English. There are also Men to the east and south, the wild Easterlings and cruel Haradrim, who follow Sauron. And there are Wild Men: the Men of Dunland, just west of the lower Misty Mountains, and the "Woses" of Drúadan Forest, near Minas Tirith.

Last but not least, except in size, there are the Hobbits. Hobbits are a little people (their height ranging from two to four feet), with hair-covered and tough-soled feet, so that they seldom wear shoes. They lived in holes originally, but at the time of the story most of them build houses. They are farmers and craftsmen, with little love for complicated machines. The good life, in their view, consists largely in eating and drinking (six meals a day when they can get them), in pipe-smoking (which they invented), and in giving and going to parties. The several varieties of Hobbits live together quite amicably in a little-known region called the Shire, having a minimum of government and as little as possible to do with the world outside.

But the four Hobbits who undertake the Quest and leave the Shire encounter all the features of this outside world that I have described. And they learn something else as well, something about its past. For an account of Middle-earth calls not only for a geography and an ethnography but a *history*. As Frodo and his companions meet Faramir, or listen to the songs of the Elves and the tales of Aragorn, or take part in the Council of Elrond, they come to know the lore of Middle-earth.

They hear of three ages, each of which comes to an end with a crucial struggle against the Dark Power. At the end of the First Age, Morgoth, as it was then, was overthrown by the High Elves. The Eldar had the help, however, of some Men, who came to be called the Edain, or Fathers of Men. As a reward these Men were granted a great isle across the sea, the most westerly of mortal lands, called Númenor, or Westernesse. There they lived in great happiness, their lives enriched through their dealings with the Elves. From time to time during the Second Age, the Númenoreans established forts and permanent havens on the western coasts of Middle-earth. But Númenor began also to show pride and rebelliousness and finally, led astray by Sauron, a servant of Morgoth, had to be destroyed. Elendil and his sons, survivors of the downfall, came to Middle-earth and established the realms in exile, Arnor in the north and Gondor in the south. Arnor was later destroyed and left desolate by the forces of Sauron, and Gondor became the special target of the Enemy's wrath. The Second Age ended with a war between Sauron and the

Last Alliance (Elves and Men), in which many of the leaders of Elves and Men perished but Sauron was overthrown and passed away for a time. The network of events in which the Hobbits have become enmeshed is bringing the Third Age to its close. The influence of the Elves is fading, the Dwarves have long been plagued with dragons, the power of Gondor has been declining, and Sauron in Mordor is gathering his forces for another decisive test of strength.

The Hobbits do not only hear of the past; they also come upon more tangible reminders. On the Barrow Downs, east of Old Forest, they are overcome by the spells of the Barrow-wights and have to be rescued by Tom Bombadil, another being of great age, who is "the Master of wood, water, and hill" (1. 135). Bombadil tells them that the Downs were the site of a battle in ancient times between the Men of Westernesse and the evil king of Carn Dúm in the land of Angmar and that the place is haunted by some of the spirits of those killed at that time. We are told that "as he spoke they had a vision as it were of a great expanse of years behind them, like a vast shadowy plain over which there strode shapes of Men, tall and grim with bright swords" (1. 157). The passageways of Moria remind them of the great days of the Dwarves. The sight of the Gates of Argonath on the River Anduin, huge stone statues of the ancient kings Isildur and Anárion, fills Frodo with awe. Desolated lands and deserted forts speak of diuturnity and loss. The inhabitants of Middle-earth, C. S. Lewis says, "are at once stricken and upheld by the memory of vanished civilizations and lost splendor."[5] Those memories become particularly poignant as the Third Age draws toward the decisive struggle which will mark its end.

That decisive struggle provides the context for the fantastic events that take place in the fantasy world I have described. The pattern is that of the traditional quest. It develops in the three stages which Northrop Frye has noted as characteristic: (1) the perilous journey and the concomitant preliminary adventures, (2) the crucial struggle, and (3) the exaltation of the hero.[6] The subtitle of *The Hobbit* is *There and Back Again,* and the phrase could apply to *The Lord of the Rings* as well. In the earlier story Bilbo Baggins of the Shire had gone, at Gandalf's instigation, to help a group of Dwarves get revenge on a fire-breathing dragon named Smaug who had expropriated the treasure-hoard of the Dwarves in the caverns under Erebor, the Lonely Mountains. Of Bilbo's adventures on the way and of his success with the dragon nothing need be said here. What is important for our story is one incident—Bilbo's finding of a ring, a ring with the magical power of making whoever puts it on vanish from sight.

The Lord of the Rings opens with Bilbo, now very old, leaving the Shire and going east. He leaves the ring, his house, and various other possessions with his young cousin Frodo Baggins, whom he has adopted as his heir and who has been living with him at Bag End. But it is not until years later that Frodo learns what his ring really is and means. Gandalf makes known to him a verse ancient in Elven-lore:

> Three Rings for the Elven-kings under the sky,
>   Seven for the Dwarf-lords in their halls of stone,
> Nine for Mortal Men doomed to die,
>   One for the Dark Lord on his dark throne
> In the Land of Mordor where the Shadows lie.
>   One Ring to rule them all, One Ring to find them,
>   One Ring to bring them all and in the darkness
>   bind them
> In the Land of Mordor where the Shadows lie.

Far back in the Second Age the Elven-smiths of Eregion, controlled by Sauron, had forged the Rings of Power spoken of in the rhyme. Gandalf tells what has happened to the rings:

> "The Three, fairest of all, the Elf-lords hid from him, and his hand never touched them or sullied them. Seven the Dwarf-kings possessed, but three he has recovered, and the others the dragons have consumed. Nine he gave to Mortal Men, proud and great, and so ensnared them. Long ago they fell under the dominion of the One, and they became Ringwraiths, shadows under his great Shadow, his most terrible servants" [1. 60].

But the One Ring, which he forged himself and into which he let a great part of his power pass, Sauron lost. It was found by one of the little people, probably of Hobbit-kind, a creature named Déagol. But his friend Sméagol murdered him for the Ring, discovered its magical properties, and ever after wandered in loneliness, wrapped up in his fierce joy over his "Precious." Because of his muttering and the strange noises he made in his throat he came to be called "Gollum." It was in Gollum's cave in the Misty Mountains that Bilbo came upon the Ring.

Gandalf tells Frodo of Sauron's preparations for war. But, he adds, "the Enemy still lacks one thing to give him strength and knowledge to beat down all resistance, break the last defences, and cover all the lands in a second darkness. He lacks the One Ring" (1. 60). He now knows (Gollum having been in Mordor) that the One Ring has been found again, and he has even come to associate it with Hobbits and the Shire. In order to save the world from this ultimate peril, Frodo must take the Ring and somehow put it beyond the grasp of the Enemy forever. This is to be his heroic Quest.

He and his neighbor Samwise (Sam) Gamgee and two young friends, Meriadoc (Merry) Brandybuck and Peregrin (Pippin) Took, set out eastward and come—after many perilous encounters with the terrifying Ringwraiths—to Rivendell and the Council of Elrond. Here are gathered representatives of all the Free Peoples— Elves of Mirkwood, Dwarves from the north, Men of Gondor, and Hobbits from the Shire—to talk about what is to be done against the power of the Dark Lord. All the strands are drawn together in another mysterious rhyme, one which came in a dream to Faramir of Gondor:

> Seek for the Sword that was broken:
>   In Imladris it dwells;
> There shall be counsels taken
>   Stronger than Morgul-spells.
>
> There shall be shown a token
>   That Doom is near at hand,
> For Isildur's Bane shall waken,
>   And the Halfling forth shall stand [1. 259].

Imladris is Rivendell. The Sword is Narsil, which broke under Elendil in the battle against Sauron and is now in the possession of his heir, Aragorn, who has become known to the Hobbits as the

Ranger named Strider. Isildur's bane is the Ring. And the Halfling is the Hobbit Frodo. All these are tokens indeed that "Doom is near at hand." The decision of the Council is that the Ring must be taken to Orodruin, the Fire-mountain in Mordor where it was forged, and cast into the Crack of Doom. Frodo volunteers. "I will take the Ring," he says, "though I do not know the way" (1. 284).

The members are chosen for the Fellowship of the Ring. Besides the four Hobbits, Gandalf, and Aragorn, there are Legolas, an Elf from Mirkwood, Gimli, a Dwarf from the Lonely Mountain, and Boromir, a son of the Steward of Gondor. The Nine Walkers are to go forth against the Nine Riders. When the sword of Elendil has been forged anew and renamed Andúril, they set out southward.

It is an often hazardous, only occasionally triumphant journey, marked by the loss in Moria of Gandalf, dragged into the abyss by the fearful Balrog; the time of rest and healing, for the survivors, among the Elves of Lóthlorien; the breaking of the Fellowship, through Boromir's treachery, at Amon Hen; the capture of Pippin and Merry by the Orcs, their escape, and their meeting with Tree-beard the Ent; the return of Gandalf, his meeting with Aragorn, Gimli, and Legolas, and the victory which they, with Théoden, King of Rohan, win over Saruman and the forces of Isengard; Sauron's siege of Minas Tirith, in which Gandalf and others of the Nine enable the Men of Gondor to triumph over not only Orcs and Men and huge machines but even the horrific winged Nazgûl; and the ordeal of Frodo and Sam, guided by the treacherous, obsessed Gollum, in bearing the Ring to Mount Doom in Mordor.

But there, on the brink of the chasm, Frodo cries out, to Sam's horror: "I have come. But I do not choose now to do what I came to do. I will not do this deed. The Ring is mine!" And he sets it on his finger and vanishes. At that moment Gollum rushes forward, wrestles with the unseen Hobbit, bites off Frodo's ring finger, loses his balance, and falls, wailing "Precious!" into the abyss. The Dark Tower falls, the hard-pressed Men of the West at the northern gate of Mordor suddenly find themselves victorious, and Frodo and Sam are rescued from the destruction of Mount Doom by the great eagle Gwaihir the Windlord.

Then follows the (very extended) "happy ending." The heroes are exalted, Aragorn enters Minas Tirith as its long-promised king, and he is married to Arwen Evenstar, the daughter of Elrond. After a leisurely journey home the four Hobbits come again to the Shire. But everything is changed, as a result—they learn later—of the influence of Saruman and the compliance of certain weak-spirited Hobbits. The returned heroes lead a rebellion. The Shire is restored to its former state, and Sam, Merry, and Pippin become of considerable importance to its life. Frodo, however, is relatively inactive and is frequently ill. Finally, two years after their return, Frodo joins the "Last Riding of the Keepers of the Rings," making his way, with the aged Bilbo and several of the Elven folk, westward to the Grey Havens and then across the sea. Sam, Merry, and Pippin bid him farewell and return together to the Shire. The Third Age has come to an end.

The very act of writing, or reading, a bare "plot summary" such as this reveals how much more Tolkien's story is than its "plot." What lifts it above mere popular fantasy fiction, what elicits a response beyond simple excitement and closer to authentic wonder, is a certain tone and a certain aura of significance which are felt to surround the fantastic figures and their adventures. Professor Frye and his disciples have taught us to account for much of this sense of import by identifying such figures as archetypal and such stories as mythic. And it is clear that Tolkien does draw his material from sources close to their roots in ritual and myth.

One notices, for example, that many of the names for the Dwarves are taken from the *Eddas*. Tolkien's conception of the Elves, furthermore, is obviously close to that of the northern myths and legends; his are the Elves of Light, exceedingly fair, lovers of light, kindly disposed toward mankind. The story itself parallels in many ways Richard Wagner's *The Ring of the Nibelung* (Northrop Frye once described Tolkien's work as a "High Anglican version of Wagner's Ring-cycle").[7]

We detect a more generalized archetypal resonance in certain images which take on a function reminiscent of motifs in primitive religions. Light at times is more than just the diffused glow that emanates from good or desirable things. It becomes the concentrated light, in a blaze or a shining surface, which communicates a sense of glory and splendor. Of the reappearance of Gandalf from the dead we read:

> His hair was white as snow in the sunshine; and gleaming white was his robe; the eyes under his deep brows were bright, piercing as the rays of the sun; power was in his hand. Between wonder, joy, and fear they stood and found no words to say [2. 98].

Not only are there magic forests and gardenlike woods in *The Lord of the Rings;* there is also a symbolic tree, meant to suggest, perhaps, Yggdrasill, the World-tree of Norse mythology. In Minas Tirith, before the Court of the Fountain where once the White Tree grew, there has for years been only a withered tree, symbol of Gondor's decline. The newly crowned Aragorn, standing with Gandalf on Mount Mindolluin, desires a sign of hope for his reign. Gandalf points to a place at the stony edge of the snow where a lone sapling grows, bearing "one small cluster of flowers whose white petals [shine] like the sunlit snow." They both recognize it as "a scion of the Eldest of Trees," and Gandalf reminds Aragorn that "though the fruit of the Tree comes seldom to ripeness, yet the life within may then lie sleeping through many long years, and none can foretell the time in which it will awake" (3. 250). It is clearly meant to have the import which Mircea Eliade ascribes to the tree in the history of religions generally—it is a symbol of the living cosmos, endlessly renewing itself.[8]

Similarly, when one reads of the huge black stone of Erech, where the Dead gather, one is reminded of the Black Stone in the Ka'aba in Mecca and other great stones, many of them possibly meteorites, which have been taken to be sacred. The effect of the incident at Erech, however, lies not so much in the feeling about the stone as in the fear and reverence felt for "the mighty dead," as Gerhardus van der Leeuw calls them. Van der Leeuw points out that Nordic and Icelandic sagas especially afford marvelous examples of the horror and devastating power emanating from the dead. The power is felt to be in their living-dead forms with their shadow life; though their form dwindles, their will is thought to be enhanced.[9]

Aragorn, moreover, is given some of the qualities of kingship which once gave that office sacred power and meaning. His kingly status is revealed in a series of "epiphanies." He authenticates his claim for the people of Minas Tirith by displaying powers of healing. His coronation inaugurates a new—a "messianic"—age.[10] Gandalf is in many respects a "savior"-figure—in his saving acts of magic power, of course, but even more in his death and resurrection at Khazad-dûm and his reappearance in glory to Aragorn, Gimli, and Legolas.

But the modern reader's imagination cannot be said to respond to the exploits of a Gandalf in precisely the way a more primitive mind would respond to the stories about the tribe's savior-king. This is not canonical myth but mythopoeic literature; the author has created a story which speaks with something of the authority of the old myths—but only with something analogous to that authority. Tolkien, I am saying, does not "believe in" Gandalf so much as he believes in something that Gandalf represents. Ultimately, the "seriousness" of "serious" fantasy lies not in the fantastic symbols as such but in the conceptions to which they—however ambiguously— refer. Which implies that our response to literary myth will be to some degree that which is appropriate to the allegorical mode. Tolkien himself speaks of the fairy story (or fantasy) as having three faces:

> the Mystical towards the Supernatural; the Magical towards Nature; and the Mirror of scorn and pity towards Man. The essential face of Faërie is the middle one, the Magical. But the degree in which the others appear (if at all) is variable, and may be decided by the individual story-teller.[11]

This "world" of fantasy which activates our sense of wonder also radiates intimations of significance. Its "natural" environment points to creative and destructive forces which are "natural" to our existence in the world. The sudden snow on Caradhras speaks to Aragorn of the "many evil and unfriendly things in the world that have little love for those that go on two legs, and yet are not in league with Sauron, but have purposes of their own" (1. 302). As symbols of other aspects of evil, the Balrog which drags Gandalf down and Shelob, the spider who stings Frodo, have the kind of capacity to suggest things like death and despair without explicitly personifying the concepts which we find also in the Maleger episode in book 2 of *The Faerie Queene*. Someone like Treebeard, on the other hand, although he too is "not altogether on anybody's *side*," makes it clear that the Orcs and their masters are creatures whose side he is "altogether *not* on" (2. 75–76). The Ents have become the allies of Men, Gandalf says to Théoden, because "not only the little life of Men is now endangered, but the life also of those things which you have deemed the matter of legend" (2. 155). There seems to be in Tolkien's "world" not only a kind of "natural evil" but also (and deeper) the kind of residual goodness and health which Irenaeus and others have believed to be present in the whole life of the physical universe through the immanence of the eternal Word.[12]

The Free Peoples of Middle-earth—Elves, Dwarves, Men, and Hobbits—along with the wizard Gandalf may be thought of as representing the rational-moral nature of man. As William Blissett suggests, if one employs the language of allegory, which is the "indispensable critical shorthand" for a discussion of the technique of composite characterization: "Frodo and his company . . . together comprise the complete hero." They are aspects of mankind and of the self manifesting their essence.[13] The relations between Men or Hobbits and the Elves seem to imply an original innocence and a primordial unity (with Nature, for example, and with the "other world") which is now fading, as Elves become increasingly a matter of legend. The Dwarves are man the maker, the craftsman, the lover of beautiful objects, not having fellowship with the earth but rather using its resources.

The feelings the Hobbits have about Men suggest that the Men of Gondor and Rohan stand for our heroic past or for the capability of that kind of heroism which in modern life is so seldom demanded. The elegiac tone of their songs bespeaks the keen awareness of mortality and tragedy which heroic passion entails. As for the Hobbits, they seem to represent "ordinariness" and the unheroic, mind-ing-one's-own-business element in man. Reunited in Minas Tirith, Pippin and Merry—forgetting Merry's recent narrow escape—are engaging in light chatter and getting ready for a pipe or two, when suddenly Pippin reflects: "Dear me! We Tooks and Brandybucks, we can't live long on the heights." Merry agrees. "But at least," he adds,

> we can now see them and honor them. It is best to love first what you are fitted to love, I suppose; you must start somewhere and have some roots, and the soil of the Shire is deep. Still there are things deeper and higher; and not a gaffer could tend his garden in what he calls peace but for them, whether he knows about them or not. I am glad that I know about them, a little [3. 146].

Comparatively unheroic though they are, the Hobbits have a certain world-affirming courage and toughness. They can rise to, if not live upon, the heights.

Gandalf's presence and powers remind us that the heights to which one must rise in order to conquer the evil represented by the Ring are inaccessible to Men and Hobbits alike without help from the "outside," without—so to speak—grace. Gandalf has come to Middle-earth from "outside," subordinate to something beyond himself yet with great gifts of power at his disposal. As Pippin shouts when the White Rider suddenly appears to rescue Faramir before the gates of Minas Tirith: "Gandalf! He always turns up when things are darkest" (3. 83).

The dark things with which the members of the Fellowship of the Ring are confronted include Sauron, the Ringwraiths, Saruman, and Gollum. These, it would seem, represent aspects of moral evil. They are characterized as the opposite of everything desirable: they are darkness, over against light; animality, against humanity; and shadow, against substance. Sauron, who in Middle-earth is the supreme embodiment of evil, is himself merely a servant or emissary. Are we to say, in view of these facts, that the Dark Power is an ultimate principle? At the very least one must say that Tolkien struggles against this Manichaean vision. "Nothing was evil in the beginning," Elrond is made to say. "Even Sauron was not so" (1. 281). The Ringwraiths were originally Men of Númenor. Saruman was

"Saruman the White," the greatest of the wizards, before he was beguiled by Sauron and began to wear robes woven of all colors. Gollum originally was probably of Hobbit-kind; and even now there can come moments when, racked by a pang of good will, he seems just "an old weary hobbit, shrunken by the years" (2. 324).

Evil is presented, in short, as a perversion of good. Often it is even a parody. Treebeard points out to Pippin and Merry that Orcs are only counterfeits of Elves. And Frodo says:

> "The Shadow that bred them can only mock, it cannot make: not real new things of its own. I don't think it gave life to the orcs, it only ruined them and twisted them; and if they are to live at all, they have to live like other living creatures" [3. 190].

Evil represents, further, a privation of being. It is always the Dark *Shadow;* its blackness is the privation of light, its shadowiness the privation of substance. Its most fearful emissaries are the winged Nazgûl, wraiths whose black robes cover nothingness.

Nevertheless, although it is not "real," evil is powerful. Its power lies in the evil will, and it is manifested in the several "falls" which are narrated or dramatized in *The Lord of the Rings* or in the appendixes. In the Second Age a king of Númenor named Ar-Pharazôn was induced by Sauron (whom he had brought as a prisoner to Númenor) to violate the "Ban of the Valar," which forbade the Men of Westernesse to sail west out of sight of their own shores or to attempt to set foot on the Undying Lands. Sauron's was the familiar argument, that "everlasting life would be his who possessed the Undying Lands, and that the Ban was imposed only to prevent the Kings of Men from surpassing the Valar." But, Tolkien declares in an appendix,

> when the king set foot upon the shores of Aman the Blessed, the Valar laid down their Guardianship and called upon the One, and the world was changed. Númenor was thrown down and swallowed in the Sea, and the Undying Lands were removed for ever from the circles of the world. So ended the glory of Númenor [3. 315, 317].

Earlier yet, even Elves had fallen under the evil influence of the Dark Lord. The Elven-smiths of Eregion were betrayed by their eagerness for knowledge into divulging the secrets of their craft, enabling Sauron to "forge secretly in the Mountain of Fire the One Ring to be their master" (1. 255). The treachery of Saruman, the corrupting of Boromir, and the prideful rejection by Frodo himself of his mission of renunciation—these are other manifestations of the power of evil.

But these examples bring us to the question of the symbolism of the Ring and the meaning of the Quest. The Ring has to do, of course, with power; but with a specific kind of power, power over the wills and the destinies of other creatures. This is, as the verse puts it, the "One Ring to rule them all." To seek such power is to usurp a right that God himself relinquishes, that of overriding freedom; therefore, the ring is inherently evil, not merely capable of being misused. The one who does use the Ring, instead of being the possessor of its power, becomes possessed by the power that made it. There is only thing to do—repudiate that kind of power absolutely. The Ring must go back to the primordial fire.

The Quest seems a strange one. "Bilbo went to find a treasure," Frodo protests, "there and back again; but I go to lose one, and not return, as far as I can see" (1. 75). But the responsibility is his, and he accepts it. The Shire has taken its peace and safety for granted, not realizing, as C. S. Lewis puts it, that "its existence depends on being protected by powers which Hobbits forget against powers which Hobbits dare not imagine."[14] We, along with the Shire-dwellers, must acknowledge the truth of Gildor's words to Frodo: "The wide world is all about you: you can fence yourselves in, but you cannot for ever fence it out" (1. 93). And we must listen, with Éomer of Rohan, to Aragorn's declaration that one must now choose for or against the Enemy; for "none may live now as they have lived, and few shall keep what they call their own" (2. 36).

Choosing *is* involved, for Tolkien's story makes it emphatically clear that we are free to choose. Even wizards are forbidden "to seek to dominate Elves or Men by force or fear" (3. 365). In the high seat on Amon Hen, the Hill of Seeing, Frodo is granted a vision of all that is going on in Middle-earth. But then, because the Ring is on his finger, he feels the Eye and its fierce eager will. Two powers are striving in him, one urging him to defy (or is it to surrender to?) the Dark Lord, the other to take off the Ring. He is aware, however, of something else also—himself, "Frodo, neither the Voice nor the Eye: free to choose, and with one remaining instant in which to do so" (1. 417).

The fact that a Hobbit or a Man has freely and responsibly taken up his appointed task does not, however, give him any grounds for pride. One must do his duty not only freely but also humbly. The Tolkien "hero" is no Achilles or Beowulf or Siegfried. Sam, having taken the Ring from the apparently dead Frodo, is tempted by it with wild fantasies of power. What holds him firm in that hour, Tolkien tells us, is not only the love of his master but also, deep down in him, "his plain hobbit sense." He knows "in the core of his heart that he [is] not large enough to bear such a burden" (3. 177). One's limitations are not to be transcended by heroic passion but humbly accepted.

But with responsibility and suffering comes growth. It is this genuine growth, along with humility, that enables the Hobbits at the end to come down from "fairy-tale" heroism to the more ordinary task of "scouring the Shire." As Tolkien argues in his essay on *Beowulf* (answering the objection that after the deeds in Heorot, Beowulf "has nothing else to do"): "Great heroes, like great saints, should show themselves capable of dealing also with the ordinary things of life, even though they may do so with a strength more than ordinary."[15]

The same development makes possible an even more difficult response: to endure the real loss which comes as a result of the wholehearted struggle against evil. It is true, as Gandalf says, that "the evil of Sauron cannot be wholly cured, nor made as if it had not been," so that "much that was fair and wonderful shall pass for ever out of Middle-earth" (2. 155). There is grim irony in the fact that one of Sauron's fingers is missing—cut off by Isildur when he seized the Ring—and that after Mount Doom the hero of the lays of victory is "Nine-fingered Frodo." But Frodo has wounds more serious than that one—so much so that he can no longer enjoy the Shire but must with the Elves and Bilbo leave Middle-earth and find his peace across the Sea. He explains to Sam: "I tried to save the Shire, and it has been saved, but not for me. It must often be so, Sam, when things are in danger; some one has to give them up, lose them, so that others may keep them" [3. 309].

The significance of *The Lord of the Rings,* however, is to be found not primarily in the dialectical alignment of its figures and forces but in the dynamic pattern of its action. Our critical concern must be not only with *what* we come to know but also with *how* we come to know it; we ask not just what the Quest is about but whether it can succeed. This brings us, first of all, to questions of narrative technique.

Basically, the "point of view" from which the story is told is that of the Hobbits. We are meant to see things their way—as the ordinary coming to know the heroic, the everyday encountering the supernatural, the uninvolved becoming involved, and the weak and fearful wondering about their chances. But this "point of view" is not a rigidly restricted one. Tolkien offers a good indirect explanation of his method by way of a conversation between Frodo and Sam about tales of adventure. One of the subjects is happy endings. Sam notes that not all the people in tales go on to a good end—and then he adds a distinction: "At least not to what folk inside the story and not outside it call a good end." Frodo agrees, and points out that he and Sam have no way of knowing what sort of tale they have "fallen into." And that's the way, he goes on, of a real tale. "You may know, or guess, what kind of a tale it is, happy-ending or sad-ending, but the people in it don't know" (2. 321). We as readers, I am suggesting, are "inside" the story with Frodo and Sam and the others, but we are also "outside" it, inasmuch as we always know much more at any point than any character in the story does. "Inside" or "outside" the story, the main question is whether or not a happy ending is possible, whether or not there is, in the struggle against evil, any ground for hope.

Those "inside" the story hear many exhortations to hope and also receive or discover several tokens of hope. Two of the gifts which the Lady of Lórien bestows on the members of the Fellowship of the Ring are such tokens: the flashing green stone, set in a silver brooch, for Aragorn and Frodo's small crystal phial. "In this phial," says Galadriel, "is caught the light of Eärendil's star, set amid the waters of my fountain. It will shine still brighter when night is about you. May it be a light to you in dark places, when all other lights go out" (1. 393). A sentence about Eärendil in an appendix exposes the depths behind this token: "Eärendil was not permitted to return to mortal lands, and his ship bearing the *silmaril* was set to sail in the heavens as a star, and a sign of hope to the dwellers in Middle-earth oppressed by the Great Enemy or his servants" (3. 314). In the desolation of Mordor, Sam also finds a star to be a sign of hope:

> Far above the Ephel Duath in the West the night-sky was still dim and pale. There, peeping among the cloud-wrack above a dark tor high up in the mountains, Sam saw a white star twinkle for a while. The beauty of it smote his heart, as he looked up out of the forsaken land, and hope returned to him. For like a shaft, clear and cold, the thought pierced him that in the end the Shadow was only a small and passing thing: there was light and high beauty for ever beyond its reach [3. 199].

"Inside" the tale, with Frodo or Sam, the reader feels their anxiety about the outcome, sees the signs, and hears the exhortations and reproofs. But from his higher point of vantage, "outside," he discerns heartening *patterns,* as well. Now, it must be understood at this point that the reader is to receive Tolkien's work imaginatively as a kind of analogy to history. The reference to "sources" such as the "Red Book of Westmarch" and the "Book of the Kings" of Gondor, the supplementary chronicles and genealogies in the various appendixes, and other comparable devices strengthen this impression. The patterning I have alluded to constitutes, then, something like a conceptual model for understanding history—not a philosophy, however, as it turns out, but a theology of history.

First, there is clearly a "providential" design, a sense of the interrelatedness of all the elements in this "history" and of an ordering of all these elements to one end. How does the Ring come to Frodo in the first place? There is "something else at work," Gandalf tells Frodo, "beyond any design of the Ring-maker." In fact, "Bilbo was *meant* to find the Ring, and *not* by its maker. In which case you also were *meant* to have it" (1. 65). What part is played in the Quest by the monomaniacal Gollum? He, too, is an unwitting instrument of Providence. Gandalf feels from the beginning that Gollum is bound up with the fate of the Ring. When Gollum has overtaken the Ring-bearers, Frodo makes their relationship explicit: "It is my fate to receive help from you, where I least looked for it, and your fate to help me whom you long pursued with evil purpose" (2. 248).

This raises, of course, the question of freedom and points to the apparent paradox of Providence, by which God creates freedom and yet dares to preordain the consummation. The historian Herbert Butterfield insists that we must think of history as though an intelligence were moving over the story, taking its bearings afresh after everything men do and making its decisions as it goes along. The proper "model" for thinking about the historical process, he suggests, is not a spiral, nor a mechanistic system, nor a growing organism, but a composer, "who composes the music as we go along and, when we slip into aberrations, switches his course in order to make the best of everything."[16]

The organization in this apparently haphazard and sporadic activity can be seen only retrospectively by those who are immersed in the stream of history, or from "above" by those who are enabled to transcend it. "You may know . . . what kind of a tale it is, . . . but the people in it don't know." Frodo freely volunteers to take the Ring to Mordor. Elrond says at once: "This task is appointed for you, Frodo." Boromir's defection is carefully presented as a free act and the breaking of the Fellowship which ensues as a catastrophe. Yet Frodo and Sam are able to enter Mordor chiefly because the Eye is busy with Aragorn and the others. The very thought of the focusing of such superlative intelligence as that of Sauron on a purpose so utterly evil as his brings dismay to the defenders of the West. But Gandalf sees in that concentrated evil a disabling defect of imagination.

> That we should wish to cast him down and have *no* one in his place is not a thought that occurs to his mind. That we should try to destroy the Ring itself has not yet entered into his darkest dreams. In which no doubt you will see our good fortune and our hope [2. 100].

Gollum is simply after his "Precious"; but without his guidance the Ring-bearers could not have reached Mount Doom. And when Frodo willfully refuses to throw the Ring into the flames, it is

Gollum's equally willful act which brings the reign of Sauron to an end. "Let us remember," Gandalf had said, "that a traitor may betray himself and do good that he does not intend" (3. 89).

Those who are "inside" the tale are able to hear some of this providential counterpoint; but they, like us, require interpreters: Gandalf, Elrond, the Lady Galadriel, and others. The revelation of a providential working strengthens in the members of the Fellowship something which is analogous to faith. Faith is tried, John Baillie has pointed out, when it is confronted by events in which it is difficult to believe there is any divine meaning. Yet other significant encounters yield assurance even for these "opaque" encounters. These, says Baillie, are "paradigmatic experiences," historical events which themselves teach us something *about* history.[17] Frodo and his companions do not know what is going to happen; only a doctrine of fate would require that. The doctrine of Providence, on the other hand, although it does not enable us to know what will happen, lets us know what it will be about, what the issues are, and "at least reassures us that we are going to have some effect upon what is going to happen."[18]

But *The Lord of the Rings,* as "history," is more than day-to-day, ongoing history. It is the history of the *end;* it is eschatology. It has to do not primarily with faith but with hope. Critics who have noticed the eschatological dimension of the work have assumed too readily that because *The Lord of the Rings* has so many other affinities with "northernness," it also embodies a northern eschatology, that it is a re-creation of the world and the world-view of *Beowulf,* communicating a sense of predetermined downfall and calling for the heroic courage of despair.[19] There is some of this in Tolkien: Denethor's despair, the battle-madness of Éomer, the sheer dogged courage of Frodo as he approaches Mount Doom. One recognizes at times, also, the characteristic elegiac tone, the deep sense of transitoriness. But the decisive battle brings no *Ragnarök;* the "twilight" is not for any gods but for Sauron and his forces. As Van der Leeuw insists, the two eschatologies are antithetical. In the *Ragnarök* the gods are defeated, in the Christian conception God triumphs. *Ragnarök* means that the world passes on to its end; for the Christian, God brings the world (or the age) to an end.[20] No, the theme is hope, not despair, and the eschatology is not "northern" but biblical. Tolkien's "myth" of the end parallels, in many important respects, the sense of the end in the biblical mythos.

Biblical eschatology, first of all, is continuous with the doctrine of Providence; that is, faith in the ultimate divine control over the whole of history issues in hope also for the consummation of all things. Both beliefs presuppose, furthermore, certain notions about *time*. The fact that in *The Lord of the Rings* we hear of three "ages" makes it clear that time, in this analogical world, does not mean mere chronological succession or inevitable evolutionary progression. On the other hand, these "ages" are not "cycles," either. There is no mythological pattern of eternal recurrence; at the most there are typological patterns. For each age constitutes a kairos, a time of opportunity and fulfillment. It is a time-with-a-content, sent for a purpose and demanding an appropriate response. Thus history as a whole is not an impersonal process but a matter involving personal will and freedom; and it consists of a continuum of "times," each with its own specific character and significance.[21]

> "Other evils there are that may come [says Gandalf], yet it is not our part to master all the tides of the world, but to do what is in us for the succour of those years wherein we are set, uprooting the evil in the fields that we know, so that those who live after may have clean earth to till. What weather they shall have is not ours to rule" [3. 155].

By the time Frodo obtains the Ring, the "weather" of the Third Age is already threatening. What is coming, Gandalf hints, is a decisive struggle of cosmic scope. This is, of course, the imagery of biblical eschatology: the end is a crisis, not an apex. This time of the End is characterized by apostasy. Boromir, Denethor, and especially the traitor Saruman represent for Tolkien's myth this falling away. It is also a time of intense suffering for the faithful, who are often drawn toward despair. The chief instrument of their torment and of the apostasy is—in the language of the Christian Apocalypse —a kind of antichrist, which the biblical scholar H. H. Rowley characterizes as an "individualizing of opposition in the figure of a monster of iniquity, who will treacherously attack his weak and unsuspecting neighbors, but who will be smitten and destroyed by the power of God in a resounding disaster."[22]

The "resounding disaster" which overtakes Tolkien's "antichrist," Sauron, is the work of a kind of composite hero: Gandalf, Aragorn, and Frodo. Gandalf has the power and Aragorn the kingly status of the rider upon the white horse in the nineteenth chapter of Revelation. Frodo's part in Sauron's downfall turns our attention away from the apocalyptic images; for here Tolkien suggests that the world is saved, ultimately, not just by grace as overwhelming presence and power but by grace as humble redemptive suffering. But when Frodo's task is done, it is Aragorn to whom our eyes turn.

Aragorn, the anciently promised, long-awaited king, is a sign incarnate, a constant reminder that there is glory yet to be, "when the King comes back." For years, while he lived in the house of El-rond, his origins were kept secret from him and he went by the name Estel (Hope). Then his identity was revealed, and he went out into the wild as a "Ranger," laboring for thirty years in the cause against Sauron. The Hobbits meet him as the Ranger named Strider. Through various "epiphanies," they come to know his full nature and status. They learn that he is heir of Isildur; then, in Lórien, they hear his new name, Elessar, the name foretold for him. Soon he is manifested as "a king returning from exile to his own land" (1. 409). They see his power. Not only is he strong in battle-courage and in wisdom; he is also—as Legolas and Gimli witness—King of the Dead. At Minas Tirith he fulfills another fragment of ancient lore—"The hands of the king are the hands of a healer"—by bringing back Faramir, Éowyn, and Merry from the brink of death. When the White Crown is placed upon Aragorn's head, it seems to all that he has been revealed now for the first time. The descriptive imagery is "messianic":

> Tall as the sea-kings of old, he stood above all that were near; ancient of days he seemed and yet in the flower of manhood; and wisdom sat upon his brow, and strength and healing were in his hands, and a light was about him. And then Faramir said:
> "Behold the King!" [3. 246].

Even more significant as a basis for hope is the pattern of happenings which we see developing—a series of unexpected rescues, of lesser "happy endings" prefiguring the ultimate triumph. Tom Bombadil's rescue of the Hobbits from the Barrow-wights fills them with "the delight of those that have been wafted suddenly from bitter winter to a friendly clime, or of people that, after being long ill and bedridden, wake one day to find that they are unexpectedly well and the day is again full of promise" (1. 155). The list of similar deliverances is a long one: Old Forest, the River Bruinen, Mount Caradhras, Fangorn, Helm's Deep, Isengard, Pelargir, the gates of Minas Tirith, the Pelennor Fields, Cirith Ungol, the Black Gate of Mordor, Mount Doom. In every one of these, despair is abruptly transformed to joy by a sudden and unexpected display of power. This can be a power seen in Tom Bombadil, or Elrond, or Treebeard, or Aragorn. But it is seen most often and most dramatically in the wizard Gandalf.

As we have seen, wizards came to Middle-earth out of the Far West as messengers sent to contest the power of Sauron. They came in the shape of Men and were thus in certain respects limited; yet "they had many powers of mind and hand" (3. 365). It is these powers that are seen in the many rescues. But the power at work in Gandalf performs one supreme, unheard-of miracle, and this becomes the sign of signs, the profoundest basis for hope. In Khazad-dûm the Balrog drags Gandalf down "far, far below the deepest delvings of the Dwarves," where "the world is gnawed by nameless things" of which even Sauron does not know, for they are older than he. Then Gandalf in turn pursues the Balrog to the highest peak, Durin's Tower in the pinnacle of the Silvertine, and casts him down. Finally darkness takes him; Gandalf dies. But he comes back from the dead and, after a time of healing in Lothlórien, reappears to Aragorn, Legolas, and Gimli. "Gandalf!" Aragorn cries. "Beyond all hope you return to us in our need!" (2. 98). "The Dark Lord has Nine: But we have One, mightier than they: the White Rider. He has passed through the fire and the abyss, and they shall fear him. We will go where he leads" (2. 104). And Pippin, close to despondency in Minas Tirith, says: "No, my heart will not yet despair. Gandalf fell and has returned and is with us" (3. 39).

The hope which Aragorn and Merry feel "in the tale" (and which we, "outside," feel *for* Frodo and Sam), a hope in large part based on the unhoped-for return of Gandalf, is clearly analogous to the hope which the Christian bases on God's mightiest act, the resurrection of Jesus Christ. Gandalf, then, parallels the *Christus Victor* of "classical" Christology, a conception rooted in the apocalyptic image of the Son of man, coming in power and glory and winning the victory over the devil and his powers. The death of this Christ would be not primarily the Son's offering a sacrifice to the Father but his entering the darkness where man is imprisoned and freeing him by defeating the primal enemies, sin and death.[23]

The Lord of the Rings, considered allegorically, speaks not only of the nature of the struggle against evil, the inescapability of involvement, the fact of freedom, the qualities of heroism, and the possibility for real loss. It also declares the viability of hope. It has a "happy ending." Frodo and Sam, their Quest achieved, wake in the sweet air of Ithilien. They see Gandalf again, and their other friends. They hear themselves acclaimed: "Long live the Halflings! Praise them with great praise!" They are seated in exaltation upon the throne of Aragorn. A minstrel of Gondor begins to sing the lay of Frodo and the Nine Fingers and the Ring of Doom. And then Sam, we are told, "laughed aloud for sheer delight, and he stood up and cried: 'O great glory and splendor! And all my wishes have come true!' And then he wept" (3. 232). This is the happy ending, indeed, what Tolkien has termed the *eucatastrophe.* And such a "sudden, joyous 'turn'" gives a fleeting glimpse of a joy which goes beyond the sense of wonder aroused by successful fantasy. It is analogous to the joy in the birth of Christ, which is the *eucatastrophe* of man's history, or in the resurrection, which is the *eucatastrophe* of the story of the incarnation. "It may be," says Tolkien, "a far-off gleam or echo of *evangelium* in the real world."[24]

But, someone protests, there is in *The Lord of the Rings* no real religion, no real God. And this is true, aside from a few enigmatic hints. Confronted with the Balrog, Gandalf announces himself as "a servant of the Secret Fire, wielder of the flame of Anor" (1. 344). An appendix tells us that when the rebellious King Ar-Pharazôn "set foot upon the shores of Aman the Blessed, the Valar laid down their Guardianship and called upon the One, and the world was changed" (3. 317). This is as close as we come in Tolkien's work to the idea of a God. Yet the *patterns* of providential ordering and eschatological crisis are there. What is important religiously in this work is not a faith *in* a "God" who orders all according to his will but a faith *that there is* such a providential design; not a hope in a God who at the end brings all things to their consummation but a hope that the happy ending will come.

It looks, in fact, as if Tolkien is being careful to exclude from his "world" almost all the machinery of orthodox piety. There is in *The Lord of the Rings* something like what Tolkien claimed to see in *Beowulf*. He points out in his Gollancz Memorial Lecture of 1936 that in *Beowulf* as we have it we can see signs that a "conversion" of the old materials had been taking place. Paganism is still there, especially in the figure of Beowulf himself. Hrothgar, however, "is consistently portrayed as a wise and noble monotheist, modelled largely . . . on the Old Testament patriarchs and kings." The narrator himself knows both the newer Christian poetry and the older heroic verse and can contemplate the new faith and learning and the native tradition together. Tolkien suggests that the author, having such a historical perspective, tended to *suppress* both the old gods and the specifically Christian references. But he kept the monsters and the heroic-elegiac tone, for "a Christian was (and is) still like his forefathers a mortal hemmed in a hostile world." "The language of *Beowulf*," Tolkien concludes, "is in fact partly 're-paganized' by the author with a special purpose."[25]

It appears that *The Lord of the Rings*, too, has been partly "re-paganized" by its author with a special purpose. C. S. Lewis was also "repaganizing" when he shifted from traditional allegorical devices to science-fiction "gimmicks" and the re-creation of myth. But of our three authors J. R. R. Tolkien seems most reliant on analogy and least given to allusion. Occasionally he will underscore the analogical relation. This may be done in the kind of "universalizing" statement attributed to Aragorn in answer to Éomer's question "How shall a man judge what to do in such times?" "As he ever has judged," Aragorn replies. "Good and ill have not changed since yesteryear; nor are they one thing among Elves and Dwarves and another among Men" (2. 41). In the appendix called "On Translation," after discussing the problem of Orc-speech, Tolkien falls again to analogizing: "Much the same sort of talk can still be heard among the orc-minded; dreary and repetitive with hatred and contempt, too long removed from good to retain even verbal vigor, save in the ears of those to whom only the squalid sounds strong" (3. 412). The most pointed reference comes in the foreword, where Tolkien presents his work to "Men of a later Age, one almost as darkling and ominous as was the Third Age that ended with the great years 1418 and 1419 of the Shire long ago" (1. 8).

But for the most part Tolkien simply allows the pattern of the action to suggest its own analogies. He, like Lewis, apparently believes in the essential truth or rightness of the imagination. A person's response to the qualities of a fairy story can bear a real relationship to his response to the revealed story of man as created in God's image and redeemed through Jesus Christ. With that confidence and with his awareness of the modern man's skepticism about things Christian, he turns to "repaganizing"; for—to quote Lewis again—"paganism is the religion of poetry through which the author can express, at any moment, just so much or so little of his real religion as his art requires."[26]

The Lord of the Rings, although it contains no "God," no "Christ," and no "Christians," embodies much of Tolkien's "real religion" and is a profoundly Christian work. Tolkien requires no "God" in this story; it is enough that he suggests in it the kind of pattern in history which the Christian tradition has ascribed to the providence of God. Aragorn and Gandalf need not turn our thoughts specifically to the Christ of Christian faith; but they persuade us that if we are to have hope in our lives and in our history, it must be hope *for* the kind of power and authority revealed in Aragorn the king and *on the basis of* the kind of power revealed in Gandalf's "miracles" and in his return from the dead. Frodo is not a "Christian"; but what Frodo does and undergoes speaks to us of what a man's responsibility, according to the Christian faith, must

E

always be—to renounce the kind of power which would enslave others and ourselves and to submit to that power which frees us to be all that we are capable of being.

As for the theme of hope—Tolkien does not commit himself to any propositions about the God who is the ground of hope or the Christ who is its content. He is satisfied to work out a kind of "phenomenology of hope." By analogy, through the images of fantasy, he suggests its "structure" in our experience: hope as it "appears" to us, with other concerns—metaphysical and theological—"bracketed." What is it like to face the approaching end and yet experience hope? It is like encountering personal will rather than dealing with impersonal process. It involves something more like a decisive battle than a continuous development, something cataclysmic rather than gradual. It requires involvement in events, not detached contemplation. It reckons with real, malignant evil, not merely ignorance or imperfection. It presupposes an ordering of the historical process to some end. And it comes to be based on "signs" and "paradigmatic events" within that history. Thus, Tolkien has created an imaginative framework—nothing more explicit than that —for the Christian experience of hope.

Needless to say, this theory has not satisfied my protest-ant reader. The delightful fantasy he read has been turned into Christian eschatology; Gandalf and Aragorn have become aspects of the Christ-event; the new age of Middle-earth is seen as the promised Kingdom; and the whole thing is a strategy for insinuating into the modern mind a Christian imagination of the possibility for hope. "That is not what *The Lord of the Rings* is," he says; "that is not it, at all."

He may simply be saying that Tolkien has written not an allegory but a "myth." Earlier I used myth and allegory as terms which are not mutually exclusive and insisted that the intimations whispered by the archetypal motifs of the trilogy are intimations of meaning, that this is a mythical allegory. Now I must place the same terms in opposition. To say that Tolkien's work is myth *rather* than allegory is to notice, for one thing, that it contains a good deal of "unassigned" imagery, in contrast to the one-to-one correspondence between symbol and concept toward which allegory tends. I have tried, even in my most flagrant allegorizing, to suggest this built-in ambiguity. Who is to say what the Ents "stand for," or Elves, or Aragorn's journey by way of the Paths of the Dead, or even the casting of the Ring into the Fire? As C. S. Lewis has said, the primary appeal of myth is to the imagination; its "indirect and further appeal to the will and the understanding can therefore be diversely interpreted according as the reader is a Christian, a politician, a psycho-analyst, or what not."[27] There are intimations of significance; but "a myth points, for each reader, to the realm he lives in most. It is a master key; use it on what door you like."[28]

There is another sense, too, in which one may want to say that Tolkien has created myth. This has to do not with the quality of the imagery in the work but with the quality of the imagination that created it. Owen Barfield says flatly:

> The modern poet has created a new myth or made a true use of an old one, according as the myth in question is the direct embodiment of concrete experience and not of his *idea* of that experience—in which case he has only invented an allegory, or made an allegorical use of a myth, as the case may be.[29]

In his *Beowulf* lecture Tolkien, unknowingly and beforehand, was arguing the case of his own fiction. Myth, he asserts, means

> becoming largely significant—as a whole, accepted unanalyzed. . . . It is at its best when it is presented by a poet who feels rather than makes explicit what his theme portends; who presents it incarnate in the world of history and geography, as our poet has done. . . . For myth is alive at once and in all its parts, and dies before it can be dissected.[30]

J. R. R. Tolkien has done precisely this—he has presented "what his theme portends . . . incarnate in the world of history and geography." Reading *The Lord of the Rings,* we are conscious first of a new world, of its geography and history, its inhabitants and its mysteries. But, as I have shown, this world has also a dimension of meaning. The question is whether the themes are "incarnate," whether the "myth is alive at once and in all its parts." And the test is *style.*

One of the devices of allegory is the use of *names* which suggest the conceptions to which the symbols refer: Duessa, Sansloy, Mr. Worldly Wiseman, Vanity Fair. In *The Lord of the Rings,* too, names are important. But a name in the trilogy designates not a conception to which it refers but some attribute of a reality in which it participates. Orcs have names like Gorbag and Grishnakh; Elves are called Celeborn or Legolas and live in places like Loth-lórien; Hobbits enjoy combinations like Peregrin Took, and places in the Shire bear names like Bywater and Bag End.

Variations in *speech*-style (not to mention fragments in other "languages," such as "Elvish") also suggest the coexistence of many kinds of creatures and of several ages of history. Tolkien explains his method in his appendix "On Translation." The Common Speech, or Westron, is spoken by most of the inhabitants of Middle-earth, and is therefore "translated" into modern English. But the "translation" also hints at the variations: the rustic dialect of Sam Gamgee, the more antique and formal language of Gondor and Rohan, the ceremonious speech which the courteous Hobbits sometimes fall into when they are addressing Elves or kings of Men.

Imagery communicates the mythic "feel" of this world. Here, for example, is how the menace of Old Forest "comes alive" for the Hobbits:

> Suddenly Frodo himself felt the drowsiness attack him. His head swam. There now seemed hardly a sound in the air. The flies had stopped buzzing. Only a gentle noise on the edge of hearing, a soft fluttering as of a song half whispered, seemed to stir in the boughs above. He lifted his heavy eyes and saw leaning over him a huge willow-tree, old and hoary. Enormous it looked, its sprawling branches going up like reaching arms with many long-fingered hands, its knotted and twisted trunk gaping in wide fissures that creaked faintly as the boughs moved. The leaves fluttering against the bright sky dazzled him, and he toppled over, lying where he fell upon the grass [1. 127].

We listen to Pippin trying to describe what it was like to look into the eyes of Treebeard the Ent:

> One felt as if there was an enormous well behind them, filled up with ages of memory and long, slow, steady thinking; but their surface was sparkling with the present: like sun shimmering on the outer leaves of a vast tree, or on the ripples of a very deep lake. I

don't know, but it felt as if something that grew in the ground—
asleep, you might say, or just feeling itself as something between
root-tip and leaf-tip, between deep earth and sky had suddenly
waked up, and was considering you with the same slow care that it
had given to its own inside affairs for endless years [2. 66–67].

In these "reaching arms" and the "many long-fingered hands," in
the "something between root-tip and leaf-tip," we find imagery used
not to personify concepts but to "humanize" an object in nature like
the old willow or to "naturalize" the quasi-human Ent. The language
creates a realm in which there is traffic between the natural and the
human, between the present and primordial time, between symbol
and concept, just as there tends to be in the primitive myth-making imagination.

Such imagery also evokes an elemental response. Consider some
of Frodo's first impressions of Lothlórien:

> Frodo looked up and caught his breath. They were standing in
> an open space. To the left stood a great mound, covered with a
> sward of grass as green as Spring-time in the Elder days. Upon it,
> as a double crown, grew two circles of trees: the outer had bark of
> snowy white, and were leafless but beautiful in their shapely naked-
> ness; the inner were mallorn-trees of great height, still arrayed in
> pale gold. High amid the branches of a towering tree that stood in
> the centre of all there gleamed a white flet. At the feet of the trees,
> and all about the green hillsides the grass was studded with small
> golden flowers shaped like stars. Among them, nodding on slender
> stalks, were other flowers, white and palest green: They glimmered
> as a mist amid the rich hue of the grass. Over all the sky was blue,
> and the sun of afternoon glowed upon the hill and cast long green
> shadows beneath the trees [1. 364–65].

This is the language of what C. S. Lewis called "stock responses,"
deliberately organized attitudes, as opposed to the direct free play of
experience. All is color—gold, white, blue, green (even the shadows
are green)—simple and strong, associated with good and desirable
elemental things. Similes and metaphors evoke other archetypal objects of reverence or sanctioned desire: "a double crown," "shapely
nakedness," "flowers shaped like stars." The whole passage is an example of the "art of enriching a response without making it ec-
centric, and of being normal without being vulgar."[31]

This elemental world and the events that take place in it come to
us in a convincing way, finally, because they come largely through

impressions which the Hobbits receive. When the author wants us to share Frodo's suspicion, in Moria, that the Nine are being followed, he first carefully shifts our attention from things seen to things heard, then, more specifically, to the footsteps of the members of the party, and finally to the stealthy Gollum.

> The Company behind him spoke seldom, and then only in hurried whispers. There was no sound but the sound of their own feet: the dull stump of Gimli's dwarf-boots; the heavy tread of Boromir; the light steps of Legolas; the soft, scarce-heard patter of hobbit-feet; and in the rear the slow firm footfalls of Aragorn with his long stride. When they halted for a moment they heard nothing at all, unless it were occasionally a faint trickle and drip of unseen water. Yet Frodo began to hear, or to imagine that he heard, something else: like the faint fall of soft bare feet. It was never loud enough, or near enough, for him to feel certain that he heard it; but once it had started it never stopped, while the Company was moving. But it was not an echo, for when they halted it pattered on for a little all by itself, and then grew still [1. 325–26].

Middle-earth and the War of the Ring, I say, are "alive" for us. They are not alive, perhaps, "in every part." Certain passages of narration seem less than convincing: the journey of Pippin and Merry with their Orc captors, the downfall of Barad-dûr, the too-lengthy celebration and homegoing, even the "scouring of the Shire"—thematically sound but dramatically a letdown. And there are stylistic lapses. Gimli's description of the Glittering Caverns of Helm's Deep is out of character (2. 152–53). Although Edmund Wilson is often simply petulant in his outrageous review, "Oo, Those Awful Orcs!" he is right in finding Tolkien too *insistent* at times on the menace in some evil creature or shuddery place.[32] Also, he sometimes tries too hard for the heroic—and archaic—ring in the speech of the Rohirrim. One wearies of the words "fell" and "fey," and of the trick of reversing word order which is so prominent in passages such as the following description of Éowyn:

> The woman turned and went slowly into the house. As she passed the doors she turned and looked back. Grave and thoughtful was her glance, as she looked on the king with cool pity in her eyes. Very fair was her face, and her long hair was like a river of gold. Slender and tall she seemed and stern as steel, a daughter of kings. Thus Aragorn for the first time in the full light of day beheld

Éowyn, lady of Rohan, and thought her fair, fair and cold, like
a morning of pale spring that is not yet come to womanhood
[2. 119].

There are certain more important respects, also, in which *The
Lord of the Rings* does not seem "alive at once and in all its parts."
These have to do, even more clearly than do stylistic faults, with
"what [its] themes portend." To begin with, a framework of fantasy
such as Tolkien's commits the writer to an emphasis on the objective
and external rather than the subjective or "inner," on force and overthrow rather than persuasion and transformation. For the philosopher Gabriel Marcel, in contrast, "hope is essentially"

the availability of a soul which has entered intimately enough into
the experience of communion to accomplish in the teeth of will and
knowledge the transcendent act—the act establishing the vital regeneration of which this experience affords both the pledge and the
first-fruits.[33]

What is largely missing in Tolkien is a convincing "experience of
communion" and all that this implies. As I have pointed out, if the
Christology implied in the figure of Gandalf is "classical," such a
Christ liberates man by defeating death and the devil, he does not
woo man's heart through moral goodness and suffering love. Man's
moral agency, furthermore, tends to become moral passivity; the
power is not within but without, and one submits rather than initiates. Hope arises not so much on the basis of certain qualities in a
relationship as on the basis of arbitrary supernatural acts. Grace—to
put it even more abstractly—is imaged not as persuasive personal
relationship but as quasi-physical force, a concept which is always in
danger of dissolving away the *moral* character of God.[34]

This is not to deny, of course, the dangers in the other tendency
of thought about grace, dangers of Pelagian self-dependence, anxious
moralism, the eclipse of the eschatological by the ethical. But, in any
case, that "model" for conceiving the relation of grace and nature
simply does not find a place, analogically, in the world of Gandalf's
staff, the Phial of Galadriel, *lembas* and *miruvor,* trees that march
off to battle, and the Rings of Power. The kind of theological bias
just described correlates with the kind of literary fantasy we have

discovered Tolkien's work to be. At this point, therefore, it might be useful to remind ourselves of what *cannot* be done with Tolkien's themes within this literary framework—not necessarily as a negative criticism of his work but as a suggestion of how, and how not, to read it.

Little can be intimated about the constructive use of power. The Kingdom is coming, not a-building. Power is something you submit to if it is good and resist if it is evil. Technological power, for example, does not come off well in *The Lord of the Rings*. Treebeard complains of Saruman that "he is plotting to become a Power. He has a mind of metal and wheels; and he does not care for growing things, except as far as they serve him for the moment" (2. 76). One of the signs of Sauron's work (through Saruman) which the returned Hobbits see in the Shire is the trees felled and the houses destroyed to make room for "the new mill in all its frowning and dirty ugliness: a great brick building straddling the stream, which it fouled with a steaming and stinking outflow" (3. 296).

Nor can one expect to see in this story the gradual reformation of persons through moral choice and persuasive grace. Tolkien brings his story to a strange climax on Mount Doom, when Frodo repudiates his mission and sets the Ring on his finger. This is, in one sense, an affirmation of freedom, the freedom to say no (*posse peccare*). It also reveals the fact, however, that Frodo has not developed, or has not been brought, to the point of being able not to succumb (*posse non peccare*). What Gollum does is a vindication both of his freedom to pursue his own evil will and of an overruling Providence which exercises its freedom in his willful act. The upshot is that Frodo here seems not to be free to do either good or evil. Tolkien has chosen to emphasize one side of the paradox of grace and freedom, giving the last word to an overriding grace.

Tolkien's literary statement of the possibility of hope, finally, is of necessity mythological and futuristic. It can hardly embody any sort of "realized eschatology." It cannot suggest, in other words, that the End *has* come, that the *eschaton* is now a matter of actual experience, a quality of life in the already present New Age.

To ask for such emphases would be, of course, to demand a radically different literary work. In concluding this chapter, however, it is better to recall and be grateful for what Tolkien *has* given us in *The Lord of the Rings*. He has taken us, first, into the enchanted world of Middle-earth and its inhabitants. That world lingers, as sights and sounds, in the memory. One remembers the radiance and the fresh, poignant colors of Lothlórien; the penetrating brown-and-green eyes of Treebeard; the Dead—"shapes of Men and of horses, and pale banners like shreds of cloud, and spears like winter-thickets on a misty night" (3. 61–62)—following Aragorn; and the snow-white hair, gleaming robes, and bright piercing eyes of the risen Gandalf. One continues to hear the muffled *doom, doom* of the mysterious drumbeats in Moria, the mad muttering of Gollum, the great horns of Rohan "wildly blowing," and "the sigh and murmur of the waves on the shores of Middle-earth" which Sam heard and which "sank deep into his heart" (3. 311).

These, and many other things seen and heard by the imagination, also tease us with intimations of import, so that we begin to entertain various possibilities of meaning. The shape of the thematic pattern which emerges corresponds to certain segments of the tradition of Christian thought. Sauron, the One Ring, Aragorn and Gandalf, the Ring-bearers, the moment of crisis at the Black Gate and on Mount Doom—all these speak of such theological concerns as the nature of good and evil, the problem of power, human freedom and responsibility, and the resources of grace. What the reader experiences, imaginatively, with Frodo and the others is analogous to the structure of the Christian experience of hope. This is hope based on the conviction of a general providential pattern in events and the memory of certain unique "paradigmatic" events; and it is hope for a "happy ending" in the future.

But what Tolkien has created is not the rigid one-to-one allegory which this summary may suggest. It yields a much "freer" experience of meaning, not easily formulable propositions but haunting hints of significance. Meaning and belief are *included* in the reception of the vivid image which has been presented to the imagination. I have tried to sketch the shape of the general pattern of belief implied in these images, not in such a way, I hope, as to "dissect" the myth and thus do it to death, but in such a way as to enrich our appreciation of its complex life. To see *The Lord of the Rings* only as an allegory of Christian hope is to see it for less—much less—than what it is. Not to see it thus at all is to see it for something *other* than what it is.

And it is also to miss much of its contemporary relevance. Our times have seen huge, destructive concentrations of economic power. Totalitarian regimes have come near to controlling not only the outward circumstances but the very wills of their people. In more subtle and more socially accepted ways men have used the powers of the mass media to manipulate human desires. Always in our minds lurk the nightmare images of hydrogen bomb devastation. And still we see leaders—"ours" as well as "theirs"—standing, as it were, upon the very Crack of Doom and preparing to put on the Ring. It is not surprising, then, that "the peculiar problem of our own day," as the English philosopher of religion Langmead Casserley declares, "is the widespread death of hope, a prevalent feeling that the end of all things is indeed at hand, unrelieved by any faith that this at the same time means that the Kingdom of God is near."[35] The gross misuse in our time of immensely augmented powers is simply a fact. The widespread death of hope is also a fact. But so is the enthusiastic response to Tolkien's parable of hope—whether one attributes this to persistent wishful dreaming, or to residual Christianity, or (as Edmund Wilson does) to "a lifelong appetite for juvenile trash."[36] This juxtaposition of facts may itself be a "sign" of some sort. For it is specifically to our world of waning hope, according to his foreword, That J. R. R. Tolkien presents *The Lord of the Rings*: "to Men of a later Age, one almost as darkling and ominous as was the Third Age that ended with the great years 1418 and 1419 of the Shire long ago."

CONCLUSION: FANTASY AND THE "MOTIONS OF GRACE"   CHAPTER 4

The notion of fantasy as the art of creating an "other world" is not, of course, original with J. R. R. Tolkien. Beginning in the eighteenth century a number of critics came to speak of the literary work in general as a heterocosm, a second nature created by the poet in an act analogous to God's creation of the world. This analogy was then developed in two related but distinct ways. It began to replace traditional ideas of the poem as "imitating" nature or as communicating knowledge about the world with the concept of the poem as an "object-in-itself, a self-contained universe of discourse, of which we cannot demand that it be true to nature, but only that it be true to itself." At the same time, certain Romantic writers, in revolt against the narrow Neoclassical definition of probability, were heard to insist that the poet's creativity resides peculiarly in his nonrealistic inventions, in the "marvelous," when through the power of imagination the poet creates what seem to be entirely new beings and new worlds.[1]

In the early ventures into the theory of prose fiction, it was this question of probability that gave rise to the distinction between a "novel" and "romance." A novel differs from Romance, according to Sir Walter Scott's formulation in 1824, because its events "are accommodated to the ordinary train of human events, and the modern state of society."[2] Romance, says Henry James almost a century later, deals with "experience liberated, so to speak, experience disengaged, disembroiled, disencumbered, exempt from the conditions that we usually know to attach to it." He reinforces the point with an image:

> The balloon of experience is in fact of course tied to the earth, and
> under that necessity we swing, thanks to a rope of remarkable

length, in the more or less commodious car of the imagination. . . .
The art of the necromancer is, "for the fun of it," insidiously to cut
the cable, to cut it without our detecting him.[3]

This does not yet take us far enough. A fantasy is not simply a
story which deals with the strange, the exotic, the horrible, or the
improbable. It is, as Robert Heinlein says, "one which denies *in its
premise* some feature of the real world."[4] James's "necromancer" is
telling us that he has cut the cable and trying to convince us that our
experience is not tied to the earth after all, or not in the way we have
believed. It is in this sense that fantasy can be called, what it is for
Tolkien, the making or glimpsing of other worlds.

If the cable the fantasist cuts is that of currently respected scientific
theory, and if he extrapolates from what is to what might some day
be, we can call his fantasy "science fiction." Science fiction is "that
class of prose narrative treating of a situation that could not arise in
the world we know, but which is hypothesized on the basis of some
innovation in science or technology, or pseudo-science or pseudo-
technology, whether human or extra-terrestrial in origin."[5]

Fantasy may merely provide an exotic setting for what is otherwise
an ordinary "entertainment"—a love story, for example, or a
"western." In other cases, it functions as a postulate which liberates
certain possibilities of tone, such as the farcical or the whimsical. A
few scientific fictions confine themselves to technological prophecy,
presenting undiscovered techniques as real possibilities in an actual
universe.

These are all recognizable types of "popular" fiction. Our concern,
however, is with the question of what constitutes "serious" fantasy.
Structurally, as Paul Goodman has helped us to see, the seriousness
of a work such as *Oedipus Rex* inheres in a certain relation between
agents and actions of "being essentially involved." The vital fortunes
of the main characters clearly turn on the chief incidents, and these
characters allow themselves to be concerned with nothing but this
vital action.[6] But seriousness is something else again in, let us say,
Shakespeare's *Richard II*. Works such as this are, in Goodman's
terms, "over-determined complex actions, determined by the characters and by some relatively independent cause, such as a theory of

history or a set of social causes," implied through diction making use of systems of imagery.

> The seriousness is given by the combination of the two determinants. The characters are destroyed by the history but suffer and are pitiful as persons. There are two kinds of discovery: the discovery of the personal plight and the disclosure of the general causes.[7]

One further distinction remains to be drawn, the now-familiar one between fictional and thematic modes, in Northrop Frye's system, or—as critics of the "Chicago School" would have it—between "mimetic" and "didactic." In these terms *Richard II* would still be considered a mimetic work, but one in which the element of thought or idea has assumed considerable structural importance. When the idea becomes *determinative*—of action, of characterization, and of the peculiar power of the work—we have something in the thematic mode, something which is, broadly speaking, didactic. Then we find ourselves asking not "How will it turn out?" but "What's the point?" The incidents of such a work constitute a "story framework" or "analogous action." Instead of the mutual implication of thought and action according to the laws of probability, we have an action which might be a framework for the thoughts, a probable occasion for the thoughts, an image of the thoughts, an occasion for feelings, or the vehicle for the feelings of which the thought and action are the objects. If long, such a story framework may have an independent probability of its own. To this action and reflection upon the action is added a structure of symbols which conveys a sense of "meaningfulness," which may or may not then be given content by historical, sociological, psychological, or religious considerations. "The dreamy world of Romance," Goodman adds, "makes easier the fabrication of such a structure of symbols."[8]

Lewis, Williams, and Tolkien have all heartily disliked the label "didactic." "I've never started from a message or a moral, have you?" says C. S. Lewis to Kingsley Amis in a discussion on fantasy. Everything, he goes on, begins with images: *Perelandra* began with a mental picture of the floating islands.[9] But to argue along this line is to confuse process with product; the point is not that there is necessarily explicit didactic intention in the author's mind, but that there is implicit didactic ordering in the work. Lewis himself, in a review of *The Lord of the Rings,* imagines someone asking Tolkien: "Why, if you have a serious comment to make on the real life of men, must you do it by talking about a phantasmagoric never-never-land of your own?" And he answers, for Tolkien: "Because, I take it, one of the main things the author wants to say is that the real life of men is of that mythical and heroic quality."[10] Of his own fantasy Lewis admits that although a story never *begins* from a "message" or a moral, "it wouldn't have been that particular story if I wasn't interested in those particular ideas on other grounds."[11]

The body of work dealt with in this study, then, may be termed "didactic fantasy." As earlier chapters have shown, Lewis, Williams, and Tolkien provide a number of the items for an inventory of forms of didactic fantasy: the allegorical quest journey, the visit from another world, the dream-vision of the state after death, the voyage to another planet, the "dystopia," the myth retold, the tale of the occult-supernatural, the spiritualist-supernatural story, and (in Tolkien's work) what might be called the fantasy epic. Because of the unique religious tendency of their fiction, moreover, the work of these men also provides a "test case" for certain *uses* of didactic fantasy.

For the reader whose experience has been mostly with serious "novels," the literary other world of didactic fantasy requires some getting used to. First of all, the peculiar power of such books is bound up in a special way with the element of "story." According to C. S. Lewis, "something which the educated receive from poetry can reach the masses through stories of adventure, and almost in no other way."[12] Accordingly, the form of a fantasy by Lewis or Williams, or of Tolkien's trilogy, will be not "spatial" but "linear." The action is often swift-paced, sensational, even melodramatic. The element of time is generally handled straightforwardly[13]; in *The Lord of the Rings* there is often an almost naive meanwhile-back-at-the-ranch quality.

Characterization in didactic fantasy seems, by novelistic standards, "flat" or two-dimensional. Actually, in romance characters tend to be aligned dialectically, not by inner motivation, so that all the reader's values are with the hero and even the opposite poles of nature (winter and spring, dark and dawn, old age and youth) are assimilated to the enemy and the hero.[14] This is not to say that the beings implicated in these actions are all simply "figures," about whose fate we care nothing at all. Some "ordinariness," some recognizable and sympathetic human traits, must be imparted, for one thing, if a Ransom or a Frodo Baggins is to be our "representative" in the spiritual perils and possibilities of the other world. But, as Lewis points out, the more the fantasy tends toward myth, the less we project into the characters; they seem shapes moving in another world. They have relevance to our life, but we do not transport ourselves into theirs.[15]

What is conventionally called "setting" assumes considerable importance in works like *Perelandra* or *The Lord of the Rings*—but with a difference. In fantasy of this kind setting constitutes, in W. R. Irwin's term, "documentation"; it validates the "other world," providing a climate, languages, customs, a history, and an "atmosphere."[16] It should be made clear, however, that setting is not "documentation" in the fiction of Charles Williams. There (as well as in Lewis' *That Hideous Strength*), the "otherness" invades this world. Setting functions there, as it does generally in the romance, to furnish for that irruption both a contrasting "realistic" backdrop and a supportive "atmosphere."

In tone, didactic fantasy can never be either tragic or comic, as such. Elder Olson argues that whereas the comic mimetic artist sets before us *the ridiculous,* the comic (didactic) satirist convinces us *that something is ridiculous.*[17] Similarly, the dangers of the journey or the battle are there not so much to arouse fear and pity in us as to convince us (by analogy) that certain things are fearful and pitiable.

We are not to expect from these authors subtlety in narrative technique. Of sophisticated manipulation of point of view or passage of time there will be little more than what has filtered down into the better popular fiction. The narrative framework, after all, is usually —for reasons already established—a popular form (the adventure story, the tale of terror, the imaginary voyage) or a primitive, subliterary type (fairy story or fable). Even the apparent exceptions in technique—Tolkien's limiting himself, for the most part, to the knowledge of the Hobbits and Lewis' occasional use of "framing" devices and restricted point of view—will, upon further consideration, prove the rule. For these have to do with the apologetic use of fantasy, the attempt to awaken the possibility of faith or hope.

Style is likewise a less prominent element in these fictions than in, say, the modernist novels of a Joyce or a Hemingway. Much of the writing is straightforward, workmanlike, narrative prose. A few special problems are encountered, however, in the creation of other worlds—"translating" the talk of their inhabitants, for example, and conveying the ceremonial quality of the utterances of heroes and of other-than-human beings. More importantly, style must function at certain points to *heighten* atmosphere and tone. What is needed at these points is "authority"—a creative authority which must be sustained within the work, not by an appeal to doctrine upheld by cultural authority or to the primeval power of myth or folk tale. For in conscious literary invention, the will or intention of the writer has to take the place of the agelong and impersonal forces of folk tradition and cultural forms.[18]

Despite these significant differences from the more familiar ambience of the "realistic" novel or that of modern "symbolic" fiction, the world of didactic fantasy has its own power and fascination. The terms used most often in earlier chapters to specify that power were "allegory" and "myth"; and indeed one might say of the fantasy of Lewis, Williams, and Tolkien what Lewis remarked of the best work of George Macdonald—that it "hovers between the allegorical and the mythopoeic."[19]

A number of years ago, in a little-known essay on fairy tales, Karel Čapek drew a parallel (one which has since, of course, become almost commonplace) between the world of the fairy tale (or fantasy) and the world of dreams. Dream images, Čapek maintains, are discontinuous, mutually irrelevant; it is when we tell the dream that we supply narrative components: "kept going," "looked around," "turned into X."[20] The images are, so to speak, the words; the narrative links constitute the syntax. Lewis says something similar. In mythical poetry

giants, dragons, paradises, gods, and the like are themselves the expression of certain basic elements in man's spiritual experience. In
that sense they are more like words—the words of a language which
speaks the else unspeakable—than they are like the people and places
in a novel.[21]

Recent research in the psychology of sleep seems to indicate that a
constraint does operate so that the memories which inhere in dream
images also "cohere in a good story." There *is* an opening up of asso-
ciative channels, however, so as to produce relations that would seem
to the waking rational mind fluid and "illogical."[22] The disconti-
nuity of dream images, which Čapek considered absolute, is more
probably relative, relative to the conscious continuity and control of
waking life. But the notion of comparative freedom of relations
among the images remains unchallenged.

In literature with an allegorical tendency, then, images resonant
of "meaningfulness" are set in motion and brought into relationship
by means of a "story framework" in such a manner that both the
qualities attributed to the images and the nature of the narrative
"syntax" will reflect the controlling influence of some apprehension
or belief.

In the writings of Lewis, Williams, and Tolkien, as we have noted
in the earlier chapters, the quality of belief approaches that of
dogmatic certainty but includes, in varying degrees, the recognition
of other possibilities for belief. Accordingly, the movement of the
narrative is analogous to the working out of a deductive argument,
with a certain amount of dialectical interplay also included. In the
fiction of Charles Williams, the dialectic is most prominent in his
earliest book, *Shadows of Ecstasy*. In Lewis it appears most clearly
near the end of his career, in *Till We Have Faces*. The work of
J. R. R. Tolkien is throughout the least dogmatic and the most
dialectical of all. Part of the pleasure of reading the fantasy of all
three men comes in watching the nice operations of the allegorical
equations, the beguiling interplay between thematic depth and fictional surface. A further satisfaction arises from the effective working
of the dialectic *within* the theme, an enjoyment related to that of
watching skillful debaters at their work. We also think about our
own experience by way of these thematic patterns. Every allegorist

wants to feel about his work what Lewis attributes to Spenser in
relation to *The Faerie Queene:* "Spenser expected his readers to find
in it not his philosophy but their own experience . . . loosened from
its particular contexts by the universalizing power of allegory."[23]

But we do not necessarily find our experience only within the
categories of the particular philosophy—or between the poles of the
particular dialectic—informing the allegorical fiction. Something else
is more deeply at work, which is associated primarily with the qualities of the *image.* Professor Tolkien ascribes to fantasy "a quality of
strangeness and wonder in the Expression, derived from the
Image."[24] In some fantasy, the didactic purpose may be subordinated
to, or generalized into, the sheer evocation of wonder. Kingsley Amis
asserts that the fantastic inventions of H. G. Wells (*The Time
Machine* and similar early works) were "used to arouse wonder,
terror, and excitement, rather than for any allegorical or satirical
end."[25]

The image can also, of course, provide escape. Tolkien takes escape
quite seriously as one of the values of fantasy. "Why should a man
be scorned if, finding himself in prison, he tries to get out and go
home? Or if, when he cannot do so, he thinks and talks about other
topics than jailers and prison-walls?"[26] Even wishful thinking is
welcomed. C. S. Lewis distinguishes, however, between two kinds of
daydreams—the Freudian wish-fulfillment dream, or "self-regarding
reverie," and another marked by the "otherness" of disinterested
imagination. The first type may be called "realistic," since it provides
the nearest substitute for real gratification. But the presence of the
second type in a story should be taken as evidence *against* the charge
that literary fantasy expresses mere wishful thinking; it may express
something more like thoughtful wishing.[27]

It is but a step from such an assertion to the suggestion that fantastic images in "serious" literature provide, not substitute gratification, but intimations of an ideal which claims selfless allegiance. The
power of allegory to evoke the image of the ideal makes itself felt
in the work of writers such as Dante, Spenser, Bunyan, and Dostoev-
ski. But the power is in the image. It is not the ideal itself, as such,
which is determining for us; it is a certain glow of otherworldliness,
of unknown possibilities of existence.[28]

It is at this point that many writers and theorists invoke the concept of "myth." Out of the long list of meanings now attachable to the term, one can find at least three which have a bearing on the content of the didactic fantasy written by Lewis, Williams, and Tolkien. A myth may be thought of, first, as a story intended to explain, for a cultural group, the relationship between an individual (or corporate entity) and the powers operating the universe. Clearly, the word is applicable in this sense to a number of the fantasies we have been considering. At one level of abstraction, "myth" can denote a general plot outline of stories serving the above purpose; e.g. the "Promethean myth." A number of Lewis' and Williams' stories incorporate such mythic patterns, especially those recorded in the first few chapters of the book of Genesis; and Tolkien's saga of the End has been considerably influenced by images and "plot structure" from biblical apocalyptic. The third significance of myth operates for these authors mainly in a negative way. If myth in this third sense can mean any explanation or assumption generally accepted by a cultural group as to how the universe "works" (the myth of progress, for example), then such myths make their way into the fiction of Lewis and Williams (and—though less so—of Tolkien) as objects for ironic and satirical treatment.

But any useful discussion of literary myth has to move beyond a concern with the *material* of myth to questions about the mythopoeic *manner* and about its effects. Structurally, literary myth is removed from the allegorical pole by ambivalent imagery; true allegory, in contrast, achieves "a rigid displacement of one aspect of the ambivalence."[29] The allegorical intention often thrusts outward toward the mythic. Lewis can thus laud a passage in the work of the late-medieval allegorist John Gower as "one of those rare passages in which medieval allegory rises to myth, in which the symbols, though fashioned to represent mere single concepts, take on new life and represent rather the principles—not otherwise accessible—which unite whole classes of concepts."[30] The thoroughly mythopoeic artist —Shelley, Blake, Kafka—will be writing the "poetry of search" (in Dorothy Sayers' phrase) rather than the "poetry of statement," will be conveying the concrete "feel" of reality rather than some abstract formula for it. "It is only while receiving the myth as a story that you experience the principle concretely. . . . What flows into you from the myth is not truth but reality (truth is always *about* something, but reality is that *about which* truth is)."[31]

Tolkien sums it up: myth means "becoming largely significant— as a whole, accepted unanalyzed. . . . [It] is at its best when it is presented by a poet who feels rather than makes explicit what his theme portends."[32]

Some of the assertions about mythopoeic literature point to the danger of a kind of *mystique* of myth. When, for example, Walter Allen categorizes the fictions of William Golding as fables, "self-contained wholes beneath whose surface action and realism are to be found much wider and, in a sense, cosmic meanings," he also recalls Golding's protest against this label:

> What I would regard as a tremendous compliment to myself would be if someone would substitute the word "myth" for "fable." . . . I do feel fable as being an invented thing on the surface whereas myth is something which comes out from the roots of things in the ancient sense of being the key to existence, the whole meaning of life, and experience as a whole.

But Professor Allen's skeptical reply must be taken with equal seriousness—"[Golding's] definition of the word 'fable' fits one's own feelings about his novels, whatever his intentions may be."[33]

The qualifying word "didactic" must still be allowed to stand. If what purports to be strict allegory can reach out toward the condition of myth, what presumes to be myth shows a corresponding tendency to assume an allegorical shape. Near one pole stands personification-allegory (as in *Everyman*), in which images, both natural and conventional, are brought into relationship in a pattern of action closely analogous to the unfolding of a deductive argument, in such a way as to set forth and reinforce a firmly held set of beliefs about the nature and destiny of man. Near the other pole might appear "literary myth," or "mythical allegory" (Kafka's *The Castle*), in which images resonating with archetypal overtones are moved about in a "plot" with the seeming arbitrariness of a dream, in such a way as to suggest all-encompassing "meaningfulness" rather than to impose a particular dogma or ideology. But at both poles, and between, it is the idea and belief in the idea (if both words are taken broadly enough) that hold sway. Through his art the mimetic poet

> attempts to bring about catharsis of spent emotion. By means of his "message," on the other hand, the allegorical poet is furthermore trying to control his audience. He seeks to sway them by magic devices to accept intellectual or moral or spiritual attitudes.[34]

Accordingly, science fiction can be said to give us the myths of our generation and can be seen as "a means of dramatizing social inquiry, . . . a fictional mode in which cultural tendencies can be isolated and judged."[35] But fantasy is put to considerably different uses in *Perelandra* or *The Greater Trumps*. One of the signs of this difference is the *sources* of the fantasy images. A science-fiction writer generally chooses a trend or a process which can be perceived in rudimentary form at the present time or imagined as attainable, and then extrapolates to its life-enhancing or death-dealing future possibilities. But Lewis and the others find their images in the literature and the folklore of the past. In *The Discarded Image* Lewis provides a vade mecum to the controlling assumptions underlying medieval attitudes and beliefs, as elicited from the writings of men like Apuleius, Alanus ab Insulis, Macrobius, Pseudo-Dionysius, and others; but he also thereby produces a partial catalogue of the creatures to be found in *The Great Divorce* and the space trilogy. Williams also has debts to Dionysius the Areopagite, but he owes even more to Dante, to Arthurian materials, and to occult lore of all ages. It is not necessary even to remark on the ancientness of the objects and beings which are met with in Tolkien's Middle-earth. In short, the other world created by these three fantasists is found to be not a world of the future at all, but an imagined realm in the past given relevance to our time or the present world made vulnerable to forces and agencies representing perennial possibilities for human existence.

These perennial possibilities are formulated in a way that generally conforms to the understanding of man in classical Christianity. Thus the quality of belief manifested in the fantasy is likely to be closer, in some respects, to that of medieval allegory than to the

indefinite symbols, the "allegorical waver" (as Professor Honig calls it), of much modern fiction. Traditional though their theology may be, however, these works are very different from their allegorical prototypes. The differences are due mainly to an awareness, shared by all three writers, of the modern cultural climate. This awareness gives rise to the "rhetoric" which everywhere affects their technique and style—the reliance on analogy, dialectic, "repaganizing," moments of "eloquence," and the rest.

Only a generalized summary of these resources is necessary at this point. The popular or naive fictional framework makes for wide appeal, camouflage of didactic intention, and (as Northrop Frye has reminded us) transparence to archetypes.[36] The interplay between unsophisticated vehicle and serious theme enlists the attention and fulfills certain expectations of the reader's intellect. The fantasy images intimate a strange world of significance while the "plot" which links the images draws the reader toward one central interpretation of the mystery. If the fantasy rises to the level of myth, so that the reader feels himself to be experiencing that mysterious reality rather than contemplating an idea of it, then the highest possible success has been attained.

In this way the imagination is "baptized" and begins to discover the "quality of the real universe, the divine, magical, terrifying and ecstatic reality in which we all live."[37] For Lewis, certain values prominent in the history of Western civilization—*Einfühlung* for nature, romantic love, *Sehnsucht*—though "sub-Christian" themselves, become the means (through the effect of fantasy) for enhancing the possibility of a Christian response to reality. Charles Williams declares that whereas superstition sees heaven and earth in the form of the beloved, for romantic theology that which is beloved can become the first preparatory form of heaven and earth.[38] For J. R. R. Tolkien (and through his art) the happy ending of the fairy story, the fulfillment of our deep desire, can be "a far-off gleam or echo of *evangelium* in the real world."[39] In all these ways—to use the words which Lewis once wrote to a friend—"any amount of theology can now be smuggled into the people's minds under cover of romance without their knowing it."[40]

If the poem is to be thought of as a heterocosm, then the poetic act must be conceived as recapitulating the original cosmogony. But which cosmogony? How does a fictional world come to be? Should it be thought of, on the Plotinian model, as an emanation from a perpetually overflowing One? At the other extreme, should we say —with Apollinaire, in the prologue to *Les Mamelles de Tirésias*— that the artist makes a world, but by sheer arbitrary fiat; that he

> no longer should reckon with time
> Or space
> His universe is the play
> Within which he is God the Creator
> Who disposes at will
> Of sounds gestures movements masses colors[41]

For theologically orthodox writers neither extreme will do. The emanationist is right, of course, to see continuity between Creator and world. C. S. Lewis can speak of God making the world "out of Himself." But this is true only in a certain sense—"in the sense that the world was modelled on an *idea* existing in God's mind, that God *invented* matter, that (*salva reverentia*) he 'thought of' matter as Dickens 'thought of' Mr. Pickwick."[42] In his Arthurian poems Charles Williams makes Nimue the energy of nature. But what that energy produces is always modeled on a pattern derived from "the third heaven," the sphere of Venus or Divine Love. "By response to that archetype Nimue brings the whole process of nature into being."[43]

This is clearly no expressionist theory of the creative act. Tolkien is very careful to speak of the process as *subcreation*. Lewis goes further yet in resisting the notion of art as self-expression. He has virtually nothing to say for "creativeness." "Our whole destiny seems to lie in the opposite direction, in being as little as possible ourselves, in acquiring a fragrance that is not our own but borrowed, in becoming clean mirrors filled with the image of a face that is not ours."[44] For Lewis, however, this "reflection" seems to be not an Aristotelian "imitation" but a Neoplatonic one. Since natural objects are themselves only imitations, Plotinus says, the arts need not simply imitate what they see but can reascend to those principles from which

Nature herself is derived.[45] *Christian* Platonism would further insist that, ultimately, adequate knowledge of these principles can come only with the aid of and in concepts provided by divine revelation. Lewis, Williams, and Tolkien create their fantasy worlds according to the true ideas or forms of the actual world which are provided for us by way of Christian dogma.

Since each of these is a world in motion, it would be better to say that each work embodies a history, or more accurately, an analogue to a particular idea of human history. Novels, says Frank Kermode, are "fictive models of the temporal world."[46] Three primary questions can be asked about this temporal movement. What *causes* contribute to it? What is the character, or *pattern,* of the movement? And toward what *end* is it directed?

The causes—in the tradition to which all three of our authors subscribe—include the divine will and human freedom. God is the summit of being, the energy in all causation, and the form of all good. Man receives his being from the Creator and is dependent upon him for his preservation in being. Man exists as rational substance in individuality and freedom. Yet in all that man causes to happen, by secondary causation, the First Cause is also at work; and man's true freedom lies in acceptance of and cooperation with the sovereign will of God. What the divine will works upon is Nature. Since God is transcendent to his creation, he must be spoken of as *super-natural*, and the modalities of his working will include such things as angels and miracles. The topic of causes can be dealt with by means of the categories of nature and the supernatural.

The pattern of the movement arises within the interplay of the nature of God's will and the nature of man's freedom. That freedom is a function of man's rationality. But as man reflects, he discovers himself existing within the limitations of space and time, and toward death. Refusing, in pride and self-love, to accept divinely ordered limits, he exercises his freedom against God and his own good. Thus his is a sinful history, requiring not only to be preserved, in divine Providence, but also to be redeemed. Redemption must take place *within* the realm of human limitation; therefore there comes to us the man Jesus, living in historicity and toward death. The power for redemption can come only from without; therefore this Jesus must also be the divine Christ, transcending time and triumphing over death. God's good will, his "grace," is made known to sinful man through revelation, primarily by means of the holy scriptures. The specific means by which salvation is brought about are secondary causes which have been supernaturalized—the church, the Bible, and the sacraments. The appropriate categories for the pattern of the movement are those of nature (specifically, fallen nature) and grace.

The Eschaton is the consummation of the will of God, for individual souls and for the cosmos, whereby existence under the conditions of time gives way to the mode of being which we call eternal life. The mysterious events and states associated with the End are spoken of as the resurrection, the Second Advent, the Judgment, hell, and the kingdom of heaven. The traditional categories under which all statements about eschatology can be subsumed are time and eternity.

In earlier chapters it has been established that this is pretty much the pattern of ideas implied in the fictional worlds of *Perelandra, Descent into Hell, The Lord of the Rings,* and the other books. It has also been suggested that while each author gives the traditional answers to all three of these questions, each one also assigns himself one question as his special field of concern. C. S. Lewis occupies himself with the question of the causes operative in the universe and the possibility of faith in the transcendent Cause. We must convince the world, he argues, that it has to choose between accepting the supernatural and abandoning all pretense of Christianity. The emphasis in Tolkien's fantasy falls on the movement of history toward an end and the possibility of hope for a good end. Williams directs our attention to the incarnational and redemptive character of life itself, so as to imbue us with the conviction that the very nature of things is love.

The traditional scheme breeds antinomies—transcendence versus immanence, foreordination versus freedom, power versus persuasion —with which every theologian (and every writer of theological fantasy) must struggle. For centuries the accepted way of dealing with each of these problems was to explore certain topics within the province of reason, others within that of faith. Certain later thinkers have been more inclined to take refuge in the notion of paradox. All have acknowledged the presence of ineluctable mystery. The fantasy images in *Out of the Silent Planet* or *The Place of the Lion* powerfully suggest this element of mystery. The handling of those images, however, often reflects a decision for one principle (transcendence, for example) at the expense of the justice done to some aspects of experience by its contrary (in this case, immanence). In varying degrees, characterization, tone, and style in these didactic fantasies reflect adversely this inability or unwillingness to maintain the tension of paradox or the depth of mystery.

But is this all that needs to be said? Do not the causes of this failure lie deeper—not in the stance of a particular author *within* the tradition but in the character of the tradition itself? It is this question which must now be explored at some length. But in what terms are the questions to be put? In recent years we have heard much concerning the failure of that tradition and concerning the questions now to be asked (and even more on those questions not to be asked). There are the theologians of the "world-come-of-age," some of whom have insisted that in the "secular city" metaphysics is dead, that questions of causes, patterns, and ends are irrelevant. Others go further yet, to announce that "God is dead" and that therefore no questions are useful which might presuppose any form of theism. One can only suggest that the negative thrust, at least, of such assertions may well be premature. The possibilities now felt in "the making of a counter-culture," as well as the continuing pressure of the not necessarily dead hand of the past, must be taken account of. Further demolition work is required, in any case, before we can fully know where the traditional project went wrong, before we can even be sure that the work of these "radical" theologians is not itself vitiated by assumptions arising out of the very tradition they claim to repudiate. More positively, the work of a few men indebted to the "new metaphysics" of thinkers such as Alfred North Whitehead—who finds the seeds for renewal by way of reexamination of the tradition itself—suggests that the task, even now, may well involve not only criticism and relinquishment but also assessment of the possibilities for reconstruction.

The theologians likely to be of most help in such a task are not the Protestant thinkers of a more or less "Neoorthodox" persuasion, inclined as they often are simply to seize upon one neglected aspect of Christian experience or dogma and reconstruct on that basis, nor the "radical" theologians, but liberal Roman Catholics such as Karl Rahner and Leslie Dewart. These men are trained, systematically and thoroughly, in the very tradition which is to be subjected to scrutiny; in that scrutiny, therefore, they are impelled toward re-examination of presuppositions, toward "the conscious historical self-fashioning of the cultural form which Christianity requires *now* for the sake of its *future*."[47] The questions aroused by the partial failure of the didactic fantasy of Lewis, Williams, and Tolkien are such as to drive us to this reexamination. There is nothing to be said against the "smuggling" of theology under cover of fantasy. But one must ask what the character of that theology is, how it correlates with the literary structure and qualities of the fantasy, and how adequate it is, finally, to the contemporary experience of reality.

As we have seen, the causes of all that happens may be categorized, in the tradition, as natural or supernatural; or, better perhaps, as secondary causes through which the First Cause operates according to their "natures" and secondary causes which have been super-naturalized. In a line of thought reaching back to Greek philosophy, nature is conceived of as the principle which necessitates, from within, the operation of beings; thus it can also refer to the particular mode of existence of any individual entity. Man acts according to (unchanging) human nature in a world of things each of which fulfills its nature, and in both man and the world the one unchanging, supernatural First Cause fulfills its purposes. Thus, Reality— on the Greek model—is not in process, but is substantially finished. As C. S. Lewis says, eloquently, in *The Discarded Image*—whereas modern man

> feels himself confronted with a reality whose significance he cannot know, or a reality that has no significance; or even a reality such that the very question whether it has a meaning is itself a meaning-less question, . . . the Model universe of our ancestors had a built-in significance. . . . There was no question of waking it into

beauty or life. Ours, most emphatically, was not the wedding gar-
ment, nor the shroud. The achieved perfection was already there.
The only difficulty was to make an adequate response.[48]

That "adequate response" is, of course, knowledge, the union of
the human mind with a reality over against it. But what man's mind
can know comes by way of its characteristic (natural) activity of
abstraction. True knowledge is in concepts, not percepts; it comes
not in the "experience" of things but in the contemplation of their
unchanging essences. By virtue of this capacity to know, man has
freedom. Reason, however, is prior to the will that exercises that
freedom. The mind fulfills its natural function when it contemplates
a concept that does justice to the nature of the thing observed; truth,
defined most broadly, is the adequation of intellect to being. The will
is truly free when it wills a thing truly known by intelligence.[49] It
is assumptions such as these which, phrase by phrase, underlie the
following characteristic assertion from *The Abolition of Man* (which
in turn parallels the novel *That Hideous Strength*):

> Either we are rational spirit, obliged for ever to obey the absolute
> values of the *Tao* [for Lewis, the moral order], or else we are mere
> nature to be kneaded and cut into new shapes for the pleasure of
> masters who must, by hypothesis, have no motive but their own
> "natural" impulses.[50]

Given this conception of nature and this understanding of man,
how are we to conceive the relations between the human and the
divine? If the integrity of divine grace is to be safeguarded, we must
postulate an order of reality "above" the natural. Christianity's assertion of a supernatural Will—Williams argues—implied no deroga-
tion from the natural, but "it did imply that that order was part of
and reposed on a substance which was invisible and which operated
by laws greater than, if not in opposition to, those which were
apparent in the visible world."[51] Certain divine attributes, then, can
be postulated simply by negativing human limitations. To say that
God is "eternal" is to say that he is not "in time." He is too *real,* says
Lewis, to have a history. "For, of course, to have a history means
losing part of your reality (because it's already slipped away into the
past) and not yet having another part (because it is still in the

future)." God neither foresees nor remembers; he merely *sees*.[52] To speak of God's omnipotence is to raise the question of the possibilities open to God (as plenitude of being) for acting upon other beings. In the fiction of Lewis, Williams, and Tolkien, fantasy often provides images of this divine omnipotence.

The supernatural operates through natural means, through secondary causes. But the relationship tends to be thought of as one-way, like "two layers laid very carefully one on top of the other so that they interpenetrate as little as possible."[53] If the natural man is even to know of grace, revelation is required. Since man is a rational being and since rationality is manifested chiefly in discourse, the locus of revelation is the propositions which constitute the divinely guided interpretation of the "faith once delivered." Faith, the means by which revelation is consummated, is an intellectual assent to the truth of revealed propositions. The object of thought here, it should be noted, is not God himself (who transcends both the human soul and that which it knows) but that which can put us on the way to God.

Language can speak of God and the divine acts only by way of analogy; man must make use of physical terms in order to denote that which at once grounds and transcends the physical. Yet the attempt can and must be made, because there is a communication of being from God to man; the Christian universe is an effect, and thereby an analogue, of God. The ultimate futility of the attempt leaves man with an unassuageable thirst. Grasping the existence of Being from his starting point of sense experience, man would become Being; but in anguish he discovers that he cannot, and thus recognizes his need, the gift of grace, and his end, the ultimate vision.[54]

It is at this point that the "Romantic Theology" held by our three authors modifies the tradition. These men turn their attention to the powers of imagination rather than those of intellect—not in order to repudiate intellect, but to complement it. For Lewis, reason is the natural organ of truth. But imagination is the organ of meaning, which functions by producing new metaphors or revivifying old ones. Just as the older tradition, then, has to presuppose the essential reliability of reason, this Romantic view implies a kind of truth or rightness in the imagination. Divine revelation finds its channel in man not merely in his intellectual hunger for truth, but in the longing of his imagination for meaning—in that sense of wonder associated with *Sehnsucht,* or the Beatrician moment, or *eucatastrophe.*

"Romantic Theology" is still, however, basically within the tradition already described. Neither truths about God nor images pointing to God are equivalent to the revelation of the living God himself. For Lewis especially the images are *mere* images: "This lower life of the imagination is not a beginning of nor a step towards, the higher life of the spirit, merely an image."[55] We are still left with analogy, even though it is now *analogia imaginationis.* The position is not far, perhaps, from that enunciated by Arthur Machen in *Hieroglyphics.* The differentia for serious literature, he first suggests, is "ecstasy," or wonder, arising out of the artist's relation to the Transcendent.

> If we, being wondrous, journey through a wonderful world, if all our joys are from above, from the other world where the Shadowy Companion walks, then no mere making of the likeness of the external shape will be our art, no veracious document will be our truth; but to us, initiated, the Symbol will be offered, and we shall take the Sign and adore, beneath the outward and perhaps unlovely accidents, the very Presence and eternal indwelling of God.

But at a later point he proposes another, quite different test: "literature is the expression, through the artistic medium of words, of the dogmas of the Catholic Church, and that which in any way is out of harmony with these dogmas is not literature"; for "Catholic dogma is merely the witness, under a special symbolism of the enduring facts of human nature and the universe."[56]

At bottom the question is whether these assumptions of Catholic dogma (even in its Romanticized form) will hold. The method of Classicism, says Charles Cochrane (comparing Greek thought with emerging Augustinian notions), was to place subject over against object and then tell a "story" (or myth) to establish an intelligible relationship between them. Such a method fails because, like a fuse in a circuit, it tends to blow out whenever the load becomes too heavy for the system.[57] The awareness of such a failure hangs heavy in the air of contemporary Christendom.

The fuse that is blowing out today—and has been in the process of doing so for three centuries—is, of course, that body of presuppositions about being and modes of being, about man and his ways of knowing, about time and eternity which came into the history of Christianity largely through the influence of ancient Greek philosophy. As Leslie Dewart remarks, theology today must be not only demythologized but also "de-hellenized."

That task can well begin with the concepts of nature and the supernatural. Nature can no longer be thought of as a static realm of "inward necessitation," but must be taken as radically contingent. It is not something inimical or resistant, to be overcome by supernatural power. It is, in short, "open"—startlingly open, to human ingenuity and divine grace. As for the "nature" of man—it can better be epitomized in the word "historicity" than the word "rationality." Consciousness is more than the mere capacity for reflection ("Man not only knows, he knows he knows"); it is "a reality which constitutes the very being of man." What takes place in the act of knowing is not the mind's union with "objective" reality, not the supplying of the merely incomplete knowledge of man with more and more truths concerning an unchanging but complex "nature." Nor is this reality "over against" man. "Man is . . . already in relation to reality whenever he exists, precisely because he is part of the world in which he exists." Man's developing consciousness is his coming-into-being. In the act of knowing, man emerges as the *sort* of reality he is; he knows *himself* in relation to reality, he is conscious being.[58] Indeed, man is always coming into being. Human existence is a project, involving change and choice. "What a man chooses in his decisions," says Rudolf Bultmann, "is basically not this or that, but is himself as the man he is to be and intends to be, or as the one who has forfeited his real life."[59]

Such a view of man assigns a new value to time, as the realm of being and truth; reality itself is timeful, historical. The most useful analogy, E. R. Baltazar suggests—in an essay on that remarkable philosopher of time and evolutionary change, Teilhard de Chardin —is that of the seed and its growth. Reality is not the seed, as a self-enclosed, self-subsisting entity, but rather the *union* of the seed with its "ground." "Substance tends to its 'other' in order *to be*," Baltazar continues. "The dynamism of being is not a having but a giving."[60] The movement in the world is not, then, nature simply becoming what it timelessly is. The world is organic, thrusting out beyond itself; one must look for directions as well as origins and expect the emergence from within the process of genuine novelty.

If the word God is ever again to be meaningful, even God himself must somehow be thought of as temporal. Eternity as mere timelessness (a notion subscribed to by Lewis and Williams) is conceivable only when one can conceive of the simultaneity of different parts of space. It is meaningless in a universe understood in terms of evolution and relativity. History must be seen, then, not as the mere unfolding of the eternal divine purpose through human instrumentality, but as the "mutual presence of God and man in the *conscious* creation of the world." The term omnipotence might well denote not what God can perform upon, or even through, "nature," but rather this radical openness of history, the "wonders that never cease" once God and man enter into personal relations.[61]

The ancient definition of truth as the adequation of intellect to being is now exposed as itself inadequate to being. One could better say that truth is—in Leslie Dewart's phrase—"the fidelity of consciousness to being." But if being, or reality, is itself in process, such fidelity is of no value apart from the structure of the particular situation. Thus truth can be further specified as "man's self-achievement within the requirements of a given situation."[62]

How, then, could God be thought of as entering into the requirements of that situation? First of all, it would have to be he himself who enters. It is dangerous to continue to insist—as C. S. Lewis does, for example—that there are "two floors" to reality; particularly when one goes on to argue, as he does, that Christ in his divine Nature, in his union with the depth of the Divine Life, never *left* that "top floor" of heaven.[63] It is misleading to speak as if there were two realms of knowledge bridged in an arbitrary fashion by divine grace. Nor does God come into the situation, so to speak, wholly "from outside." Close study of Lewis' writings reveals a number of images—man as tin soldier or statue, the world as occupied planet, etc.—stressing the transcendence of God, the utter helplessness of man, and the near-arbitrariness of the motions of grace. On the contrary, as Dewart insists, "when [God] visits the world he does not come slumming. He comes to stay."[64] However we may choose to explain his otherness, God is a reality who, in his very reality, lives "here below."

Revelation, then, is event; and it is inseparable from the whole of experienced reality. Christian theism is first of all a way of life, rather than intellectual assent to a body of dogma. Belief is imported into knowledge for the inner meaning of one's "natural" truth. But if Christian theism is a way of life, faith must be a mode of existence. Primordially, faith is "basic trust." It is, as such, openness: to oneself, to the other, to history, and to the End—and to God as present to, and involved in, all these. More specifically, faith may be defined as "a commitment of one's existential self in the light of a certain apprehension of reality as disclosed in living experience."[65] Dogma, then, is to be redefined as simply the formal means by which faith comes into being specifically as human, that is to say, as conscious. The formulation and interpretation of dogma is a process by which we render ourselves present to that in which we believe.[66] This, too, however, must be conceived of as social-historical process; the intelligibility of any belief about reality will be that of a particular time and place.

To speak meaningfully, then, about the "causes" of the movement we call human history, we must continue to rethink the term "nature" along the lines indicated by modern developments in the physical sciences, the study of history, and the sciences of man. This can be done in such a way, however, that "nature" is conceived as inclusive of, or receptive to, the mystery, the otherness, and the openness connoted by (though misleadingly) the word "supernatural." But the "causes" at work through the fantastic agencies in Lewis' fiction are modeled, by analogy, on the pattern of ideas making up traditional Christian theism. His reliance on that tradition helps to account for certain major weaknesses found even in his best work.

One feels, for example, that the author "manipulates" his characters. This is not, of course, an accusation of "two-dimensional"

F

characterization; Lewis does not write novels of character development. But if the possibility of faith is what is at issue and if faith is a mode of existence rather than simply "thinking with assent," then one requires a certain sense of freedom and a certain complexity in the main characters even of didactic fantasy. Characters in a Christian novel, says Jean-Paul Sartre (assailing Mauriac), ought to be "centers of indeterminacy," not slaves of some fake omniscience, manipulated according to an obsolete world-style.[67]

The modern reader finds also a certain one-sidedness, a lack of dialectical tension, in Lewis' books. Ideas other than the controlling ones are presented, but in such a way as to be violently overborne. The violence may find its way into the action (as in the concluding struggles of *Perelandra* and *That Hideous Strength*) or into the style (in passages of overly savage satire or incantatory eloquence). The last novel, *Till We Have Faces,* allows much more freedom of movement to systems of belief in competition with the truth. But even in that book—in the "vision-ritual" at the end—one feels the pressure of traditional supernaturalism, with its tendency to demean the natural and the merely human so as to exalt the divine holiness and power.

The controlling concern in the fiction of Charles Williams is not to bring the human individual, by way of an image of fantasy, into the presence of the supernatural Cause, but to reveal the supernatural at work *in* the natural. His fantasies point to the pattern of that movement. If Lewis works out a kind of metaphysics-by-analogy, Williams implies an ontology, "a description bearing upon structures which reflection elucidates starting from experience."[68]

Although Williams thinks with the same traditional presuppositions as does C. S. Lewis, he tries harder to reconcile the contradictions in the system. As even the title of one of his essays indicates, he has much to say about "natural goodness." For Williams, nature and the supernatural are not opposed, they are complementary. Thus he is able to say that "where love is, there is Christ; where there is human reconciliation, there is the Church." What consciousness of the supernatural should do is deepen this experience.[69]

The basis for such assertions is Williams' preoccupation with incarnation and atonement, and his concern for maintaining the

"two-sidedness" of these doctrines. Although redemption must operate from *outside* the created world, since creation cannot heal its
own wound, it must also operate from within, if the integrity of the
creature is to be preserved. On several occasions Williams seems
to go out of his way to affirm the humanity of the incarnate Word,
almost to promulgate a gospel of true secularity. Today, he says at
one point, the doctrine of Christ's manhood, with its corollaries, has
still to be worked out and put in action—in our wrestling with the
problem of a just State, the problem of marriage, and the requirement for honesty, or "accuracy," in our talk about the faith and its
relationships.[70]

His beliefs about man, too, are built upon his characteristic notion
of coinherence. Man is flesh and spirit; "Flesh knows what spirit
knows, but spirit knows it knows." Man is both reason and imagination. Knowledge comes by way of the creative reception and rational criticism of images. We seem to have, in short, a thoroughly
incarnational, sacramental idea of man and the world within a
supernaturalist framework.

But that is not the whole of the story the fiction tells. Certain expectations, as we have seen, are aroused but then disappointed. The
novels present something of the ordinary course of life which, to be
convincing, love must transfigure; but this is then subordinated to
fantastic images of love as sheer transmutative energy. The imaginative power of those images is in turn constrained by a too-rigid
pattern of believed ideas, making for a sense (as in Lewis' work) of
manipulation and exploitation. Finally, the very idea of love—love
as mutuality, as coinherence—is seen to be secondary to the ultimate
goal of vision.

The logic of traditional Christian theism has betrayed him.
Williams may assert that the manhood, in the doctrine of the incarnation, remains to be worked out. But he lays still greater stress
on that Athanasian either/or which insists that the incarnation takes
place "not by conversion of the Godhead into flesh, but by taking
of the manhood into God." He is either ignorant of, or ignores,
the possibility of a genuinely reciprocal Christology. The tradition
draws back, of course, from such an understanding of Christ, because of Hellenized presuppositions about being which lead it to

formulate the problem in terms of "natures." But the unity is not a matter of "natures" at all; it is the coincidence of divine and human acts. The question, as John Knox says, should be: "What is God doing through Christ?" For "God's action *is* the divine nature of Christ."[71]

A similar tendency can be detected—despite all his pronouncements to the contrary—in Williams' thinking about man and the conditions of his existence. Man's fleshliness is acknowledged and pronounced good, but it is somehow assumed into spirit. Temporality and historicity are also slighted in favor of the divine power and eternity. Writing about faith in the cross as a trust in what is already done, Williams says: "Not only His act, but all our acts, are finished so. . . . It is finished; we too do but play out the necessary ceremony."[72] Particularity must submit to the Idea, individual experience to dogma.

Charles Williams shares with C. S. Lewis the categories of nature and the supernatural. By his emphasis on incarnation and atonement, however, Williams manages to avoid the near-dualism in Lewis' thought. But the unity he celebrates is one attained by including the natural within the supernatural. He focuses upon the structures of the natural and derives an "ontology of love"; but he locates and interprets these structures by means of the insights available in the supernaturalist frame of reference. A statement such as "The God-bearing image does not confer revelation from above" seems to promise empiricism and secularity; however, the adversative phrase—"but raises the beholder to a vision of God in a movement from nature to that which is above and beyond nature"—defeats those expectations.[73]

But Richard R. Niebuhr is right to insist that if the biblical picture of Christ is the norm, then nature itself will include the "supernatural." Christ, rather than being determined by a prior system of nature, will be the illuminator and revealer of a "larger" system of nature.[74] The question of *how* the grace of God in Christ is present to (sinful) nature is the topic of a reformulation of the Nature/Grace problem by the Roman Catholic theologian Karl Rahner. Taking seriously the modern insistence on *experiencing*

grace (rather than simply inferring its reality or experiencing something analogous as a "pointer" to it), Rahner turns within the
Catholic tradition to a related notion, that of "glory." Grace and
glory are two stages in the one process of divinization. In glory,
what God does for the "supernaturally elevated created spirit" is
not merely to actualize his intelligence, or grant him a revelatory
vision, or "infuse" him with a special power; he communicates
himself.[75]

The possibility is dependent on the close connection of incarnation and creation. Rather than taking these as two separate acts of
God's loving freedom, Rahner suggests (with the Scotists) that "the
original act of God (which settles everything else) is his emptying
of himself, Love giving up himself, in the Incarnation, so that with
the Incarnation the order of grace is already *there*. . . ." By his free
coming into the world the incarnate Word "makes the world's order
of nature his nature, which presupposes him, and the world's order
of grace his grace and his *milieu*." He comes "unto his own."
Grace therefore is present to man's life as creature, to his existence
as well as his essence. "Man's whole spiritual life is permanently
penetrated by grace. Just because grace is free and unmerited, this
does not mean that it is rare."[76] A man does not respond to grace,
then, merely by making in the "natural" realm those acts which
direct him *toward* God's revealed mysteries. On the contrary,
Rahner concludes: "*If* in each moral act he takes up a positive or
negative position towards the *totality* of his actual existence . . .
then we should have to say that every morally good act done by a
man is in the order of salvation also a supernatural act of salvation."[77]

As even this rather traditional formulation implies, if images of
fantasy are to communicate the awareness of reality-as-love, those
images must be able to affirm the real presence of a gracious God
without negating the facticity, historicity, and freedom of man.

J. R. R. Tolkien—in contrast to Lewis and Williams—seldom
writes anything which explicitly sets forth his world-view. There are
only hints in *The Lord of the Rings,* for example, about any transcendent supernatural Cause operative in the life of Middle-earth.

Yet these hints, along with the pattern of ideas implicit in the structure of the work, would be enough to place the trilogy in the tradition also—even if Tolkien had not (as he did on one occasion) identified himself as a Christian and the world of the Ring as a "monotheistic world of 'natural theology.' "[78] Considerably more is done with the *pattern* produced by the causes. What unfolds by way of the kingly exploits of Aragorn, the endurance of unmerited suffering by Frodo, and the supernatural power of Gandalf over death and the demonic is clearly a redemptive movement.

But what chiefly concerns us in *The Lord of the Rings* is the End toward which we move. The theme is eschatology, the occurrences with which our known world comes to its end. The sense of an end broods over all of the story, beginning as early as chapter 2, where we learn that "Elves, who seldom walked in the Shire, could now be seen passing westward through the woods in the evening, passing and not returning; . . . singing sadly to themselves."[79] The feeling is elegiac, "Northern"; but the thematic concerns are Christian. We are led to ask two questions: What characterizes the time of the End, and what ought we who must live in that history to bring to its moments of crisis and decision?

For it is, first of all, a time of crisis. The dimensions of the crisis for Middle-earth only begin to be understood in book 2, with the Council of Elrond. Here representatives of the several Free Peoples learn the danger they face—no less than the destruction of all that has been built up in the Third Age—share their fragmentary knowledge of the process by which peril has grown, and make what decisions they can for countering the forces of evil. In such decisions, as Rudolf Bultmann says, "the yield of the past is gathered in and the meaning of the future is chosen."[80]

Decision implies freedom and the openness of the future. It is important, therefore, for the reader always to feel—in the world of mighty forces which we call Middle-earth—that Frodo and the others are exercising the power of free choice. The fascination of the Ring must be emphasized, and the susceptibility of its bearers. This is what makes Boromir so important to the story; and it is for this reason that Frodo is made to seize the Ring for himself at the very

moment when his mission is about to be completed. The temptation
to despair must also be given substance and weight. The reality of
hope is inseparable from that temptation, the impulse to disarm
before the inevitable, to become fascinated by our own destruction.[81]
In *The Lord of the Rings* there are, as there must be, many occasions—like the moment Frodo spends in the Seat of Seeing on
Amon Hen—in which someone is made aware of himself as "free
to choose, and with one remaining instant in which to do so" (1.
417).

The possibility of hope is also dependent upon the fact of freedom.
One chooses to go on in the face of seemingly impossible circumstances. This is not, however, a core of absurdity. The conception
of hope is symbolized and supported by all experiences of renewal.
Hope can grow, nourished by a conviction of providential ordering
and by experiences or events which image the ultimate happy ending.

Even Tolkien's fantasy, however, registers the pressures exerted
by certain constraints in the tradition. The concept of power, for
instance—prominent though it is in the story of the Ring—is a
curiously narrow one. With respect to power, we ordinary creatures
are clearly thought of as passive rather than active. The Hobbits
are mysteriously drawn into the cosmic struggle and are used by the
unseen powers. Their freedom lies mainly in their capacity to resist
evil forces and agencies. Little is said about the constructive, creative
use of power. In fact, such use of power is specifically presented as
a temptation to evil, by way of the debate between the wizards
Saruman and Gandalf in the tower of Orthanc. Power is granted
in order that one may serve the purposes of the unseen Power for
good by resisting evil and helping to preserve the good that has already been bestowed. Where reality is conceived, however, not as
substantially complete but as in process, power has to include creativity as well as preservation.

Similarly, freedom has to include not just the capacity to respond
but the power to initiate. At one crucial moment in *The Lord of the
Rings,* even that freedom of response is compromised in order that
the providential governance might be exalted. An authentic sense

of freedom is conveyed in the incidents leading up to Boromir's defection, and we are not offended by the way in which this event is later turned to the general good. But the climactic scene on Mount Doom is another matter. There Frodo's self-will and Gollum's desperate craving are both overruled by the unseen Purpose. Behind the outcome of this confrontation lurk traditional presuppositions about causation. In Providence, God orders all things in view of himself, by his knowledge and love. But he acts in all things according to the law of the species. The essence of man is rationality and freedom; therefore the First Cause acts through human (secondary) causation.[82] It would appear, however, that in this way the individual's freedom and power (to final self-determination) are affirmed only in the abstract, whereas the divine absoluteness of power (to determine the final determination of other selves) is affirmed in the concrete.

This does not begin to do justice to the human experience of freedom. In his freedom man does not simply choose this or that, the will acting as the executive of intellect. Such a position remains too close to the Greek ahistorical assumption that "man cannot really be touched by encounters, but encounters can only be for him occasion and material for unfolding and shaping his timeless nature."[83] What man actually chooses in such encounters is himself and his future.

There is more of this self-creating aspect of freedom in *The Lord of the Rings* than in the fantasies of Lewis or Williams. The Hobbits leave the Shire as "boys," so to speak; they return as "men." Frodo learns the high spiritual cost of living, in terms of pain and suffering, and develops his capacity for endurance. He even grows into acceptance of and compassion for the disgusting Gollum. Gollum himself figures in a particularly impressive moment of decision, in which he experiences the "temptation" of goodness. He unexpectedly finds Frodo and Sam asleep and at his mercy. But then, we are told,

> a strange expression passed over his lean hungry face. The gleam faded from his eyes, and they went dim and grey, old and tired. A spasm of pain seemed to twist him, and he turned away, . . . shaking his head, as if engaged in some interior debate [2. 324].

The conversation between Frodo and Sam which precedes this incident, however, contains a clue to the reason for Tolkien's final failure to render the texture of the autonomous act. When the Hobbits are talking of themselves as if they were "in a tale" and Frodo says: "You may know . . . what kind of a tale it is . . . happy-ending or sad-ending, but the people in it don't know," Sam adds: "Things done and over and made into part of the great tales are different. Why, even Gollum might be good in a tale" (2. 321-22). But we are not willing to say that we are simply *in* a tale, even one told by a loving, all-powerful God. We do not simply choose whether or not to play our appointed parts in a story already composed; we are helping to *invent* the incidents and the plot.

For medieval historiography, world history was universalistic; a comprehensive meaning was thought to be imposed by the tran- scendent divine counsel, using human instruments.[84] Modern theo- logians are inclined to see history rather as made by man, consciously created, but in the presence of God. Thus everything is possible; history is radically open. "The openness of the future to man is what allows for human freedom and creativity; the openness of the future to God is what makes history redemptive."[85]

If this is true, then the complex and far-reaching process of change which has produced our contemporary experience must not be considered simply a perversion of human nature. But if the analogies implied in the fantasy images of *The Lord of the Rings* are taken seriously, it becomes clear that Tolkien does repudiate— or wishes he could repudiate—much of what constitutes our moder- nity. The modern age cannot be imagined, for instance, apart from technology and industrialism. Even if the world is destined, through cybernetics and the mass media, to become a "global village," the basis for existence and the style of life in that "village" will be largely determined by scientific technology and the industrial economy. Now, one does not expect modern economic and social structures to be determinative of life in the Third Age. But for that very reason one finds it somewhat surprising that the author specifically contrives to express the *repugnance* he feels toward machinery, factories, and mills, especially that "tall chimney of brick" which the returning Hobbits find in the Shire "pouring out black smoke into the evening air" (3. 283). The glimpse we are given of the New Age to follow after the defeat of Sauron reinforces this general impression. That glimpse is of a great City which, we are told, in the time of Aragorn's reign

> was made more fair than it had ever been, even in the days of its first glory; and it was filled with trees and with fountains, and its gates were wrought of mithril and steel, and its streets were paved with white marble; and the Folk of the Mountain laboured in it, and the Folk of the Wood rejoiced to come there; and all was healed and made good, and the houses were filled with men and women and the laughter of children, and no window was blind nor any courtyard empty; and after the ending of the Third Age of the world into the new age it preserved the memory and the glory of the years that were gone [3. 246].

No mills or chimneys there; only trees and fountains and crafted objects of great beauty. This may be a gratifying vision of possibilities for communal human life; but the vision is achieved by excluding, rather than by incorporating and then transfiguring, the less than pleasant realities of the modern scene.

The image of that City is consonant, however, with the concept of the End in the tradition we have been examining. The End comes exclusively *to,* rather than also *from within,* human history. It comes as a judgment on the distortions resulting from the work of evil in the world and as preservation and renewal of the good which nevertheless abides. With its coming the confused motions of human history are superseded by the patterned perfection of eternity. Within the static, substantial, intellectualistic, and unhistorical categories bequeathed by the tradition, images of the End are likely to be those of destruction and preservation rather than of continuous creation, those exalting renovation rather than innovation. But there is available another model for thought. The divine power may be manifested not in the eschatological foreclosure of history's moral ambiguity but in the opening of unlooked-for possibilities.[86] The past few centuries have witnessed the emergence of new assumptions—dynamic, relational, holistic, and historical— ways of thinking which seem also to be implicit in much of the biblical picture of man and in Trinitarian notions about God. Only those images, fantastic or otherwise, which find themselves at home with such assumptions about reality can adequately express the modern man's experience of ultimate hope.

Of what "use" to us, finally, is didactic fantasy such as that written by Lewis, Williams, and Tolkien? For their purposes would they have been better advised to concern themselves exclusively with *this* world? The Tolkien phenomenon alone would stand in partial refutation of any such purely negative judgment. But beyond the prevalence of Hobbits in the imagination of modern readers, there are many things in the work of all three men which can impress their readers with a sense of its powers.

Some of their images of "other worlds"—the verticality of the Malacandrian landscape, the vivid hues of Perelandra, the forests, caverns, and waterways of Middle-earth—may aid us in perceiving afresh the wonder of *this* world; particularly if, as Lewis remarks, "something which the educated receive from poetry can reach the masses through stories of adventure, and almost in no other way."[87] Where the capacity for wonder has been attenuated through the routine and conventionality of daily life or vulgarized by the insistent mass media, we can be grateful for whatever images will help to "re-condition the public mind to mystery."[88]

As for the didactic element, their very commitment to the tradition enables these authors to expose the poverty of certain assumptions about man and the world which have arisen sheerly in reaction against the older ways of thought. They expose our chronological snobbery, the tendency to forget that our time too is only a "period." C. S. Lewis rides out—satirical lance at rest—against the world-view of shallow naturalism and against an arrogant imperialistic technology which is still very much with us. There are, after all, affinities between N.I.C.E. in *That Hideous Strength* and what we have come to call the "military-industrial complex." Charles Williams opposes to the self-centered individualism that is always among us his vision of love as the very nature of things, a vision in some ways not far from Teilhard's belief in "the hidden and eventual release of forces of attraction between men which are as powerful in their own way as nuclear energy appears to be, at the other end of the spectrum of complexity."[89] In what happens to Boromir and Denethor—and almost happens to Frodo—Tolkien exposes the destructive, inhuman outcome of hope's archenemy, despair. It could be argued that the best part of *That Hideous Strength* is the negative, satirical first half and that Lewis' best work, generally speaking, is found in the ironic satire of *The Screwtape Letters* and the self-lacerating irony of *Till We Have Faces*. As for Charles Williams, it is clear, I think, that his strongest novel, *Descent into Hell,* is also his "darkest."

There are dark things also in Tolkien's fantasy—the fog and the cold of the Barrow Downs, the tentacled creature in the pool near Moria Gate, the desolate wastes of Mordor, and the ride through the Paths of the Dead. But *The Lord of the Rings* serves chiefly to remind us that the strength of all these fantasies is meant to appear not just in moral condemnation of evil and unbelief but also in mythopoeic affirmations of the motions of grace. Any list of the triumphs of the myth-making imagination in these books—and every reader would have his own list—would have to include Ransom's first glimpse of "Space," the paradisaic landscape of Perelandra, the traffic with the realm of the dead in certain scenes of *Descent into Hell* and at the beginning of *All Hallows' Eve,* the beauties of Lothlórien, Treebeard the Ent, the reappearance in glory of the wizard Gandalf, the awakening of Frodo and Sam in Ithilien, and even (in a different tonality) the departure of Frodo for the Uttermost West.

These images of fantasy, both negative and affirmative, can serve as analogues for the mysterious motions of the human spirit (which is, as Lewis said, "the only real 'other world' we know"): for its secret desires and fears, its loathings and longings. Thus the fantasy in parts of *Descent into Hell* and in books 4 and 5 of *The Lord of the Rings* can have an effect somewhat like that of Kafka's explorations of the heart of darkness. At other times it can tap the unimagined resources out of which flow responses of faith, hope, or love. But, as we have seen, the powers both of blackness and of light are likely to be constrained by the pressures of an inimical allegorical scheme. Fantasy can be used to objectify the experience of bondage or that of deliverance. Perhaps, however, the appropriate fictional framework would be nearer that of "romance," presenting in-depth characters and authentic moral conflict and then moving into fantasy, or to the brink of fantasy—as in Saul Bellow's *Henderson the Rain King*, for instance, or *Second Skin*, by John Hawkes—for the symbols of new creation.

Fantasy can also embody the vision of various futures into which our world could move. This has been, of course, the province of science fiction and utopian fantasy. These days much fantasy of this sort finds its way into so-called "black humor." When actuality itself seems a grimly ludicrous parody of a fantasist's work, many artists find themselves driven to create even more wildly exaggerated images and even more absurd connections in order to convey some sense of conceivable future enormities. The nearest thing to futuristic "black humor" in the fantasy of Lewis, Williams, and Tolkien appears in the satirical portions of *That Hideous Strength*. But even that satire—and the eschatological motifs in *The Lord of the Rings* —demonstrate the adverse effects of inadequate notions of time and change. The hope for the world seems here to lie in restoration of the old rather than in continuous change of the kind spoken of by Teilhard, a process in which the "supernaturalizing Christian Upward is incorporated (not immersed) in the human Forward."[90]

At this point in the twentieth century one can sense still another possibility for futuristic fantasy, taking the form, perhaps, of a new species of utopian fiction. So far the full emergence of a technological society and our painful acknowledgment of historicity have been the themes chiefly of a literature of "dystopia" riddled with the revulsion and fear of a *Brave New World* or a *1984*. More recently, however, the "meta-Freudian" prophets, Norman O. Brown and Herbert Marcuse (as well as other visionaries and ideologues), have been setting forth a new interpretation of history and a new vision of the End. In "taking history seriously," Brown tells us, we have fallen into the trap of historicism. What we must come to realize is that history is part of the "universal neurosis of mankind" produced by repression. It is a nightmare from which we must awaken—awaken into eternity, "the mode of unrepressed bodies."[91] Surely it is fantasy that must supply the images for that eschatological ideal. And, indeed, there are glimpses of what such a world could be like (along with the more typical science-fiction "gimmicks") in a book much read among the young in recent years, Robert Heinlein's *Stranger in a Strange Land*.[92]

But if in the fantasy of Lewis, Williams, and Tolkien traditional dogmas about eternity and time have resulted in a distorted representation of present actuality, the new utopianists will have to guard against comparable dangers stemming from their very different ideologies. Even a neurosis has to be "worked through"; the glow of the eschatological symbol of unrepressed life must not blind us to the struggle that has to be carried on—in history—if we are to come nearer to that transformation of cultural reality which is the precondition for "eternal life."

Fantasy may function, finally, to raise the question of what is ultimate. In the words of Austin Farrer:

> Get a man to see the mysterious depth and seriousness of the act by which he and his neighbors exist, and he will have his eyes turned upon the bush in which the supernatural fire appears, and presently he will be prostrating himself with Moses, before him who thus names himself: "I am that I am."[93]

The qualities of the images invented by our three authors imply, first, an insistence on ontic categories for ultimacy. This emphasis on the "objectivity" of grace seems a salutary one, in view of the modern tendency to reduce everything to subjective experience. It might be questioned, however, whether the concept of objectivity implied in their fantasy should be—as it most often is—that which is appropriate to objects and forces. Ian Ramsey insists that in the "disclosure situation," in which God's presence becomes known, there are both subjective and objective constituents, so that cosmic disclosures reveal what is other than ourselves while being at the same time situations in which we come to ourselves and realize a distinctive subjectivity. But this is not, he insists, the objectivity of dream images, nor of physical objects and scientific causes, nor even of other "people" as the topics of social statistics. *"It is the objectivity of what declares itself to us*—challenges us in a way that *persons may do."*[94]

The kind of imaginative response required by certain images of fantasy may well provide an analogy for the beliefful relation to what is ultimate in reality. According to Kierkegaard, the Christian requirement of belief even implies a special rhetoric, a new science of "Christian oratory." Aristotle, Kierkegaard points out,

> relates the art of speaking and the medium for awaking faith . . . to probability, so that (as opposed to knowledge) it is concerned with that which can also be apprehended in a different way. Christian eloquence would differ from Greek eloquence in this, that it is only concerned with the improbable, with showing that it is improbable so that a man can *believe* it.[95]

The difficulty encountered in the fantasy of Lewis, Williams, and Tolkien lies not with belief in the improbable, as such, but with the *context* prescribed for that belief, the network of assumptions within which belief attains its general revelance.

Professor Ramsey, in *Christian Discourse,* has a good deal to say about the "qualifiers" used in talk about God, words such as "beyond," "behind," "within," "above"—"the words which save not the appearances but the transcendence." Such qualifiers, he says, function as operatives, or imperatives, providing us with "techniques of extension or subdivision or inward penetration which we are to bring to bear on our 'world' or 'perceptual field.' " In order to talk about God, then, we "develop stories about the present world .in a direction specified by the imperative 'beyond,' until a disclosure occurs whereupon 'X' is posited to refer to what is disclosed."[96] Those stories moving from actuality in the "direction specified by the imperative 'beyond' " could well include the literature of the "improbable": fantasy. One other problem obtrudes itself, however —the requirement of revelance. For revelance, says Ramsey, one turns to "models," which are taken from the contexts on which qualifiers have worked to yield disclosures. And "the most dominant model provides the best articulation."[97]

One hesitates to assert flatly that the didactic fantasy of Lewis, Williams, and Tolkien is deficient simply as a result of being bound up with a model which is no longer dominant. After all, the older image has not yet been completely discarded, and allegory can be a means of transition from one world-view to another. In that case, Lewis and Tolkien are right to insist that the "proof" of their fantasy is in the "mythic" qualities of the images themselves. This mythopoeic power is unquestionably present in the work of all three writers—occasionally in Lewis and Williams, abundantly in Tolkien. Tolkien's fantasy is superior, I think, chiefly in two respects, one having to do with the sources of the images, the other with his handling of them. I find that the exploits of Gandalf and the terror aroused by the Ringwraiths are not as convincing as the "personality" of Treebeard the Ent and the mysteries of Old Forest, the Barrow Downs, and the Paths of the Dead. Tolkien is at his best, in other words, when the sense of the "supernatural" emerges out of the "natural," as the sign of a hidden but pervasive power. He is strong, also, when the sense of meaningfulness imperceptibly flows from an accumulation of sensory details, rather than confronting us by way of a series of pointed allusions in a "purple passage."

If didactic fantasy, then, is to speak from within one world-view so as to be heard within another, its allegory will have to be tactful, offering an image with multiple possibilities of meaning. It must also be tolerant. Images must be admitted which are dissonant to the images revelatory of the controlling idea; the narrative framework will have to suggest ambiguity, perhaps even ambivalence; and characters embodying genuinely competing points of view will have to clash in dialectical give-and-take. John Bayley speaks of a "neutrality of love" whereby a great author "can make us see his characters both as we see ourselves and as we see other people."[98] In didactic literature, the equivalent of Bayley's "neutrality of love" toward characters is something like a "neutrality of justice" toward ideas. But here, as we have seen, even Tolkien falls short. The tradition itself may be largely responsible for this failure as well. For what it lacks is "a conception of truth in which substantial transformation of man's understanding of being does not necessarily imply unfaithfulness to an earlier, less well-developed stage of understanding."[99]

Even reliance on myth yields, finally, no standing place. In the terms of Frank Kermode's important distinction, "myth operates within the diagrams of ritual, which presupposes total and adequate explanations of things as they are and were." What we have more need of are "fictions," for "they change as the needs of sense making change" and thus "find out about the changing world on our behalf." Time—especially its continuity, or successiveness—remains *the* problem for the artist:

> To do anything at all he has at once intensely to consult and intensely to ignore it. . . . Ignoring it, we fake, to achieve the forms absent from the continuous world; we regress toward myth, out of this time into that time. Consulting it, we set the word against the word, and create the need for difficult concords in our fictions. But we ignore it at great peril.[100]

Too often C. S. Lewis, Charles Williams, and J. R. R. Tolkien fall victim to that peril. They do not fail because they are true to an ancient pattern of presuppositions; they fail because—one must dare to say—in that allegiance they are less than true to themselves. A man who would be true to himself must come to terms in some manner with his culture, and thus, in turn, with his history. To set aside the reality of the present in any significant degree is to reject or distort some part of oneself. The cost of that rejection may then make itself felt in the literary texture—even in the very tone—of that which is addressed to other selves. For in the enterprise of apologetics, as Archbishop Temple once warned us, "I am not asking what Jones will swallow; I *am* Jones asking what there is to eat."

The "other worlds" of fantasy created by Lewis, Williams, and Tolkien can at times expose a certain narrowness of outlook in the world we know. They can at times bring us to ponder the relevance of long-standing beliefs to some of the questions of the present. They may even help to create in the skeptical, empirical modern mind some possibility for belief in the reality of the Divine Presence; to lead the self-seeking, individualistic manipulator of things and men toward life within a coinherence contained, upheld, and given meaning by the transcendent reality of Love; and to foster within the self-reliant quester fallen into the Slough of Despond the indefeasible hope for an ultimate happy ending. When the fantasy leaves us incredulous, we discover that what we have found unbelievable is not the other world of Perelandra or that of Middle-earth or even the world of gracious possibility as such, but what has now become for us the other world of the *Consolation of Philosophy* or the *Summa*.

NOTES

Introduction

1. For biographical information about Charles Williams, see Alice Mary Hadfield, *An Introduction to Charles Williams* (London: Robert Hale, 1959); Anne Ridler's introduction to Charles Williams, *The Image of the City and Other Essays* (New York: Oxford University Press, 1958); and the preface by C. S. Lewis to *Essays Presented to Charles Williams* (New York: Oxford University Press, 1947). Useful reminiscences of C. S. Lewis are found in the memoir with which W. H. Lewis prefaces his edition of the *Letters of C. S. Lewis* (New York: Harcourt, Brace & World, 1966) and in *Light on C. S. Lewis*, ed. Jocelyn Gibb (New York: Harcourt, Brace & World, 1966). Information about Tolkien may be gleaned from William Ready, *The Tolkien Relation: A Personal Inquiry* (Chicago: Henry Regnery, 1968).

2. Northrop Frye, *Anatomy of Criticism* (Princeton: Princeton University Press, 1957); Edwin Honig, *Dark Conceit: The Making of Allegory* (Evanston: Northwestern University Press, 1959); Angus Fletcher, *Allegory: The Theory of a Symbolic Mode* (Ithaca: Cornell University Press, 1964); Frank Kermode, *The Sense of an Ending: Studies in the Theory of Fiction* (New York: Oxford University Press, 1967).

3. In books such as Nathan A. Scott's *Modern Literature and the Religious Frontier* (New York: Harper & Row, 1958); idem, *The Broken Center: Studies in the Theological Horizon of Modern Literature* (New Haven: Yale University Press, 1966); J. Hillis Miller's *The Disappearance of God: Five Nineteenth-Century Writers* (Cambridge, Mass.: Harvard University Press, Belknap Press, 1963); idem, *Poets of Reality: Six Twentieth-Century Writers* (Cambridge, Mass.: Harvard University Press, Belknap Press, 1965). Kermode's *The Sense of an Ending* may also be considered theological criticism.

4. Martin Jarrett-Kerr, *Studies in Literature and Belief* (New York: Harper & Row, 1955), p. 13.

5. D. S. Savage, *The Withered Branch: Six Studies in the Modern Novel* (New York: Pellegrini and Cudahy, 1950), p. 16.

6. J. Hillis Miller, *The Disappearance of God: Five Nineteenth-Century Writers* (New York: Schocken Books, 1965), pp. ix-x.

Chapter 1 C. S. Lewis:
Fantasy and the Metaphysics of Faith

1. *The Problem of Pain* (1940); *The Case for Christianity* (1943); *Christian Behavior* (1943); *Beyond Personality* (1944); and *Miracles* (1947).

2. C. S. Lewis, *The Pilgrim's Regress: An Allegorical Apology for Christianity, Reason, and Romanticism,* 3d ed. (London: Geoffrey Bles, 1943).

3. Dorothy Sayers, *The Poetry of Search and the Poetry of Statement* (London: Victor Gollancz Ltd., 1963), pp. 206, 216.

4. Lewis, op. cit., p. 10.

5. Ibid., p. 12.

6. C. S. Lewis, *The Screwtape Letters* (New York: Macmillan, 1943). Subsequent references will be included in the text, in parentheses.

7. C. S. Lewis, *The Screwtape Letters and Screwtape Proposes a Toast* (New York: Macmillan, 1961), p. vii.

8. Ibid., p. xii.

9. C. S. Lewis, *The Great Divorce* (New York: Macmillan, 1946). Subsequent references will be included in the text, in parentheses.

10. C. S. Lewis, *Out of the Silent Planet* (New York: Macmillan, 1943). Subsequent references will be included in the text, in parentheses.

11. C. S. Lewis, *Surprised by Joy: The Shape of My Early Life* (New York: Harcourt, Brace & World, 1955), pp. 35–36.

12. C. S. Lewis, "An Expostulation," *Poems,* ed. Walter Hooper (New York: Harcourt, Brace & World, 1964), p. 58.

13. Maleldil may be thought of as the Word, the Eternal Son, revealing the Father, the "Old One."

14. C. S. Lewis, *Perelandra* (New York: Macmillan, 1944). Subsequent references included in the text, in parentheses.

15. Victor Hamm, "Mr. Lewis in Perelandra," *Thought* 20 (June 1945): 271.

16. C. S. Lewis, *Preface to Paradise Lost* (New York: Oxford University Press, 1942), chapter 17.

17. Ibid., p. 69.

18. Ibid., p. 66.

19. C. S. Lewis, "On Stories," *Essays Presented to Charles Williams* (New York: Oxford University Press, 1947), p. 98.

20. Marjorie Hope Nicolson, *Voyages to the Moon* (New York: Macmillan, 1960), p. 251.

21. C. S. Lewis, *That Hideous Strength* (New York: Macmillan, 1946). Subsequent references will be included in the text, in parentheses.

22. Wayne Shumaker, "The Cosmic Trilogy of C. S. Lewis," *Hudson Review* 8 (Summer 1955): 254.

23. C. S. Lewis, *Letters to Malcolm: Chiefly on Prayer* (New York: Harcourt, Brace & World, 1964), p. 73.

24. C. S. Lewis, *The Case for Christianity* (New York: Macmillan, 1946), p. 50.

25. J. V. Langmead Casserley, *Toward a Theology of History* (London: A. R. Mowbray and Co., 1965), p. 155.

26. C. S. Lewis, *The Discarded Image: An Introduction to Medieval and Renaissance Literature* (Cambridge: Cambridge University Press, 1964), p. 88.

27. Lewis, "Epigraph 15," *Poems*, p. 136.

28. Clyde S. Kilby, *The Christian World of C. S. Lewis* (Grand Rapids: Eerdmans, 1964), p. 81.

29. C. S. Lewis, *Rehabilitations and Other Essays* (New York: Oxford University Press, 1939), p. 33.

30. C. S. Lewis, "Transposition," *They Asked for a Paper: Papers and Addresses* (London: Geoffrey Bles, 1962), p. 179.

31. C. S. Lewis, *Beyond Personality: The Christian Idea of God* (New York: Macmillan, 1945), pp. 64, 58.

32. Austin Farrer, "The Christian Apologist," *Light on C. S. Lewis,* ed. Jocelyn Gibb (New York: Harcourt, Brace & World, 1966), pp. 40–41.

33. Reinhold Niebuhr, *The Nature and Destiny of Man* (New York: Charles Scribner's Sons, 1953), 1:167, 169.

34. Arthur Michael Ramsey, *An Era in Anglican Theology: From Gore to Temple* (New York: Charles Scribner's Sons, 1960), p. 3.

35. Lewis, *Beyond Personality*, pp. 5, 7, 27, 35.

36. W. Norman Pittenger, "Apologist vs. Apologist: A Critique of C. S. Lewis as 'Defender of the Faith,'" *The Christian Century* 75 (1 October 1958): 1106.

37. Lewis, *Beyond Personality*, p. 26.

38. C. S. Lewis, *Miracles: A Preliminary Study* (New York: Macmillan, 1947), p. 134.

39. Ibid., p. 162.

40. Lewis, *The Case for Christianity*, pp. 47, 40.

41. Lewis, *Beyond Personality*, p. 26.

42. John Baillie, *The Idea of Revelation in Recent Thought* (New York: Columbia University Press, 1956), p. 100.

43. Lewis, *Beyond Personality*, p. vi.

44. C. S. Lewis, "On Obstinacy in Belief," *They Asked for a Paper*, pp. 185, 193.

45. Etienne Gilson, *The Spirit of Medieval Philosophy*, trans. A. H. C. Downes (New York: Charles Scribner's Sons, 1940), p. 260.

46. Lewis, *Rehabilitations*, pp. 157–58.

47. C. S. Lewis, "Myth Became Fact," *World Dominion* 22 (Sept.-Oct. 1944): 269.

48. C. S. Lewis, "The Weight of Glory," *They Asked for a Paper*, p. 208.

49. Lewis, *Surprised by Joy*, pp. 235–36.

50. C. S. Lewis, "Is Theology Poetry?," *They Asked for a Paper*, pp. 158–59.

51. Lewis, "Myth Became Fact," p. 270.

52. Lewis, *Rehabilitations,* p. 158.

53. C. S. Lewis, "Historicism," *Month* 4 (Oct. 1950): 242.

54. Lewis, "The Weight of Glory," p. 202.

55. C. S. Lewis, introduction to St. Athanasius, *The Incarnation of the Word of God* (*De Incarnatione Verbi Dei*), trans. A Religious of C.S.M.V. (New York: Macmillan, 1947), p. 7.

56. Farrer, op. cit., p. 34.

57. C. S. Lewis, ed., *George Macdonald: An Anthology* (New York: Macmillan, 1947), p. 21.

58. Lewis, "The Weight of Glory," p. 201.

59. Lewis, *Surprised by Joy,* p. 167.

60. C. S. Lewis, *Till We Have Faces: A Myth Retold* (New York: Harcourt, Brace & World, 1956). Subsequent references will be included in the text, in parentheses. Lewis also wrote fantasy, of course, between 1945 and 1956; but it consists of the "Narnia" books for children, which I have chosen not to deal with in this essay.

61. C. S. Lewis, *English Literature in the Sixteenth Century, Excluding Drama* (New York: Oxford University Press, 1954), p. 342.

62. Kilby, op. cit., p. 58.

63. Lewis, *Letters to Malcolm,* pp. 43–44.

64. Farrer, op. cit., p. 41.

65. Lewis, "Reason," *Poems,* p. 81.

66. *Light on C. S. Lewis,* ed. Gibb, p. xi.

67. Lewis, "As the Ruin Falls," *Poems,* pp. 109–10.

68. W. B. Yeats, "Anima Hominis," *Per Amica Silentia Lunae, Mythologies* (New York: Macmillan, 1959), p. 331.

Chapter 2 Charles Williams: Fantasy and the Ontology of Love

1. Although *Shadows of Ecstasy* was not published until 1933, it was written before the other novels.

2. Charles Williams, *Shadows of Ecstasy* (New York: Pellegrini and Cudahy, 1950), p. 167. Subsequent references will be included in the text by initials—*SOE*—and page numbers, enclosed in parentheses.

3. *War in Heaven* (1949), *Many Dimensions* (1949), *The Place of the Lion* (1951), and *The Greater Trumps* (1950); all New York: Pellegrini and Cudahy. Subsequent references to these books will be by initials—*WIH, MD, POL, GT*—and page numbers, enclosed in parentheses.

4. Anne Ridler, introduction to Charles Williams, *The Image of the City and Other Essays,* ed. Anne Ridler (New York: Oxford University Press, 1958), pp. xxiii-xxv.

5. Charles Williams, *Witchcraft* (New York: Meridian Books, 1959), p. 311.

6. Paul Tillich, *The Protestant Era,* trans. James Luther Adams (Chicago: University of Chicago Press, 1948), chapter 7, "Nature and Sacrament."

7. Charles Williams, *The Forgiveness of Sins,* in *He Came Down from Heaven* and *The Forgiveness of Sins,* 1-vol. ed. (London: Faber & Faber, 1950), p. 176.

8. Williams, *Witchcraft,* pp. 76–78.

9. Charles Williams, *The Descent of the Dove: A Short History of the Holy Spirit in the Church* (London: Faber & Faber, 1950), p. 58.

10. Williams, *He Came Down from Heaven,* p. 25.

11. Charles Williams, "The Index of the Body," *The Image of the City,* ed. Ridler, p. 85.

12. William Temple, *Nature, Man and God* (New York: Macmillan, 1949), p. 493.

13. Williams, *The Descent of the Dove,* p. 46.

14. Charles Williams, "Natural Goodness," *The Image of the City,* ed. Ridler, p. 76.

15. Charles Williams, *Collected Plays* (New York: Oxford University Press, 1963), p. 179.

16. Williams, *The Descent of the Dove,* p. 69.

17. Mary M. Shideler, *The Theology of Romantic Love: A Study in the Writings of Charles Williams* (New York: Harper & Row, 1962), p. 11.

18. Charles Williams, *The Region of the Summer Stars,* in *Taliessin through Logres* and *The Region of the Summer Stars,* 1-vol. ed. (New York: Oxford University Press, 1944), p. 26.

19. C. S. Lewis, "Williams and the Arthuriad," *Arthurian Torso,* ed. C. S. Lewis (New York: Oxford University Press, 1948), pp. 141–43.

20. This is the notion of perichoresis (*circumincessio*) which, according to G. L. Prestige (who applied to this concept the word coinherence), arose as a christological term for the process of unification between the two natures of Christ and then came to be applied to the Trinity. See G. L. Prestige, *God in Patristic Thought* (London: S.P.C.K., 1952), chapter 14.

21. Shideler, op. cit., p. 81.

22. Charles Williams, "The Way of Exchange," *The Image of the City,* ed. Ridler, p. 153.

23. Lewis, "Williams and the Arthuriad," p. 79.

24. Charles Williams, *Descent into Hell* (New York: Pellegrini and Cudahy, 1949). Subsequent references will be by initials—*DIH*—and page numbers, enclosed in parentheses.

25. Charles Williams, *All Hallows' Eve* (New York: Pellegrini and Cudahy, 1948). Subsequent references will be by initials—*AHE*—and page numbers, enclosed in parentheses.

26. Shideler, op. cit., pp. 169–71.

27. Williams, *He Came Down from Heaven,* p. 21.

28. Lewis, "Williams and the Arthuriad," pp. 131–32.

29. Williams, *Witchcraft,* p. 62.

30. Shideler, op. cit., pp. 115–20.

31. Williams, *He Came Down from Heaven,* p. 36.

32. Ibid., p. 60.

33. Charles Williams, "Fathers and Heretics," review of *Fathers and Heretics: Studies in Dogmatic Faith* by G. L. Prestige, *Time and Tide* (16 November 1940): 1123.

34. Charles Williams, "The Cross," *Image of the City,* ed. Ridler, pp. 136–37.

35. Williams, *The Forgiveness of Sins,* p. 124.

36. Williams, *The Descent of the Dove*, p. 235.

37. Shideler, op. cit., p. 13.

38. Charles Williams, "Malory and the Grail Legend," *Charles Williams: Selected Writings*, ed. Anne Ridler (New York: Oxford University Press, 1961), p. 160.

39. Richard M. Eastman, "The Open Parable: Demonstration and Definition," *College English* 20 (Oct. 1960): 15–18.

40. Shideler, op. cit., p. 28.

41. Williams, *He Came Down from Heaven*, p. 33.

42. Shideler, op. cit., p. 61.

43. See chapter 1, p. 7.

44. Williams, *The Forgiveness of Sins*, p. 164.

45. Ibid., p. 177.

46. Charles Williams, *The English Poetic Mind* (New York: Oxford University Press, 1932), pp. 116–17.

47. Williams, *The Descent of the Dove*, p. 25.

48. Charles Williams, *Flecker of Dean Close* (London: The Canterbury Press, 1946), p. 62.

49. Williams, *The English Poetic Mind*, p. 172.

50. L. A. Cormican, "Milton's Religious Verse," *A Guide to English Literature*, ed. Boris Ford, vol. 3, *From Donne to Marvell* (Baltimore, Md.: Penguin Books, 1956), p. 184.

51. Allan D. Galloway, *The Cosmic Christ* (London: Nisbet & Co., 1951), pp. 128, 106.

52. Williams, *The Forgiveness of Sins*, pp. 120, 132.

53. Edwin Muir, *The Structure of the Novel* (London: Hogarth Press, 1963), p. 26.

54. Eugene R. Fairweather, "Christianity and the Supernatural," *New Theology No. 1*, ed. Martin E. Marty and Dean Peerman (New York: Macmillan, 1964), p. 238.

55. *Letters of James Agee to Father Flye* (New York: Bantam Books, 1963), p. 186.

56. Williams, *The Descent of the Dove*, p. 59.

57. Shideler, op. cit., p. 69.

58. W. Norman Pittenger, *The Word Incarnate: A Study of the Person of Christ* (Welwyn, Herts, England: James Nisbet and Co., 1959), pp. 13, 92.

59. Shideler, op. cit., p. 72.

60. Fairweather, op. cit., p. 247.

61. C. S. Lewis, *Essays Presented to Charles Williams*, ed. C. S. Lewis (New York: Oxford University Press, 1947), pp. xii-xiii.

62. Williams, "The Cross," pp. 131–32.

63. Richard R. Niebuhr, *Resurrection and Historical Reason: A Study of Theological Method* (New York: Charles Scribner's Sons, 1957), p. 87.

64. Williams, "The Cross," p. 138.

65. Etienne Gilson, *The Spirit of Medieval Philosophy*, trans. A. H. C. Downes (New York· Charles Scribner's Sons, 1940), p. 286.

66. Joseph A. Mazzeo, "Dante's Conception of Love," *American Critical Essays on "The Divine Comedy,"* ed. R. J. Clements (New York: New York University Press, 1967), p. 153.

67. Nicholas Berdyaev, *The Destiny of Man* (New York: Harper Bros., Harper Torchbooks, 1960), p. 192.

68. H. R. Niebuhr, *The Responsible Self: An Essay in Christian Moral Philosophy* (New York: Harper & Row, 1963), pp. 69–70.

69. Ernest Beaumont, "Charles Williams and the Power of Eros," *Dublin Review,* Spring 1959, p. 73.

70. Roger Sale, "England's Parnassus: C. S. Lewis, Charles Williams, and J. R. R. Tolkien," *Hudson Review* 17 (Summer 1964): 210–14.

71. John Bayley, *The Characters of Love: A Study in the Literature of Personality* (London: Constable and Co., 1960), p. 39.

Chapter 3   J. R. R. Tolkien:
Fantasy and the Phenomenology of Hope

1. J. R. R. Tolkien, "On Fairy-Stories," *Essays Presented to Charles Williams,* ed. C. S. Lewis (New York: Oxford University Press, 1947), p. 70.

2. Page references (by volume and page, in parentheses) will be to the Houghton Mifflin edition (1956), vol. 1: *The Fellowship of the Ring;* vol. 2: *The Two Towers;* vol. 3: *The Return of the King.*

3. Tolkien, "On Fairy-Stories," pp. 42, 62.

4. Austin Farrer, *The Glass of Vision* (London: Dacre Press, 1948), pp. 13–14.

5. C. S. Lewis, "The Gods Return to Earth," *Time and Tide* 35 (14 August 1954): 1083.

6. Northrop Frye, *Anatomy of Criticism* (Princeton: Princeton University Press, 1957), pp. 186–87.

7. These sources have been canvassed in Lin Carter, *Tolkien: A Look Behind "The Lord of the Rings"* (New York: Ballantine Books, 1969).

8. Mircea Eliade, *Patterns in Comparative Religion,* trans. Rosemary Sheed (New York: Sheed & Ward, 1958), p. 267.

9. Gerhardus van der Leeuw, *Religion in Essence and Manifestation,* 2 vols. (New York: Harper & Row, 1963), 1: 128–31.

10. Ibid., chapter 13.

11. Tolkien, "On Fairy-Stories," p. 53.

12. Allan D. Galloway, *The Cosmic Christ* (London: Nisbet & Co., 1951), p. 106.

13. William Blissett, "Despots of the Rings," *South Atlantic Quarterly* 58 (Summer 1959): 453–54.

14. Lewis, "The Gods Return to Earth," p. 1082.

15. J. R. R. Tolkien, "Beowulf: The Monsters and the Critics," *The Proceedings of the British Academy* (New York: Oxford University Press, 1936), 22: 51–52.

16. Herbert Butterfield, *Christianity and History* (New York: Charles Scribner's Sons, 1949), pp. 108–9.

17. John Baillie, *The Sense of the Presence of God* (New York: Charles Scribner's Sons, 1962), pp. 74–75.

18. Ibid., p. 185.

19. See, for example, Douglass Parker, "Hwaet We Holbytla . . . ," *Hudson Review* 9 (Winter 1956/57): 598–609.

20. Van der Leeuw, op. cit., 2: 586.

21. For much of this I am indebted to John Marsh's article "Time," *A Theological Word Book of the Bible,* ed. Alan Richardson (New York: Macmillan, 1950).

22. H. H. Rowley, *The Relevance of Apocalyptic* (London: Lutterworth Press, 1944), p. 32.

23. Galloway, op. cit., pp. 62–63; Gustaf Wingren, *Man and the Incarnation: A Study in the Biblical Theology of Irenaeus,* trans. Ross Mackenzie (Edinburgh: Oliver & Boyd, 1959), pp. 120–22.

24. Tolkien, "On Fairy-Stories," pp. 81–83.

25. Tolkien, "Beowulf: The Monsters and the Critics," pp. 21–22, 42–44.

26. C. S. Lewis, *English Literature in the Sixteenth Century, Excluding Drama* (New York: Oxford University Press, 1954), p. 342.

27. C. S. Lewis, *Rehabilitations and Other Essays* (New York: Oxford University Press, 1939), p. 29.

28. Lewis, "The Gods Return to Earth," p. 1082.

29. Owen Barfield, *Poetic Diction: A Study in Meaning* (London: Faber and Gwyer, 1928), p. 232.

30. Tolkien, "Beowulf: The Monsters and the Critics," pp. 14–15.

31. C. S. Lewis, *Preface to Paradise Lost* (New York: Oxford University Press, 1942), pp. 54–57.

32. Edmund Wilson, "Oo, Those Awful Orcs!" *Nation* 182 (14 April 1956): 312–14.

33. Gabriel Marcel, *Homo Viator: Introduction to a Metaphysic of Hope* (Chicago: Henry Regnery Co., 1951), p. 67.

34. N. P. Williams, *The Grace of God* (London: Longmans, Green & Co., 1930), p. 6.

35. J. V. Langmead Casserley, *Toward a Theology of History* (London: A. R. Mowbray & Co., 1965), p. 222.

36. Wilson, op. cit., p. 314.

Chapter 4   Conclusion:
Fantasy and the "Motions of Grace"

1. M. H. Abrams, *The Mirror and the Lamp: Romantic Theory and the Critical Tradition* (New York: W. W. Norton & Co., 1958), pp. 272, 275–77.

2. Miriam Allott, *Novelists on the Novel* (London: Routledge & Kegan Paul, Routledge Paperback, 1965), p. 49.

3. Henry James, *The Art of the Novel: Critical Prefaces by Henry James,* ed. R. P. Blackmur (New York: Charles Scribner's Sons, 1953), pp. 33–34.

4. Basil Davenport, et al., *The Science Fiction Novel: Imagination and Social Criticism,* 2d ed., rev. (Chicago: Advent Publishers, 1964), p. 23; italics mine.

5. Kingsley Amis, *New Maps of Hell: A Survey of Science Fiction* (New York: Harcourt, Brace & World, 1960), p. 18.

6. Paul Goodman, *The Structure of Literature* (Chicago: University of Chicago Press, 1954), pp. 26, 28.

7. Ibid., pp. 63–64.

8. Ibid., pp. 220–24.

9. "Unreal Estates: On Science Fiction—C. S. Lewis, Kingsley Amis, Brian Aldiss," *Encounter* 24 (March 1965): 62.

10. C. S. Lewis, "The Dethronement of Power," *Time and Tide* 36 (22 October 1955): 1374.

11. "Unreal Estates," p. 62.

12. C. S. Lewis, "On Stories," *Essays Presented to Charles Williams,* ed. C. S. Lewis (New York: Oxford University Press, 1947), p. 102.

13. Williams' *Descent into Hell* constitutes something of an exception; its emphasis on character development and its treatment of sequential time identify it as approaching the condition of "romance" rather than that of fantasy.

14. Northrop Frye, *Anatomy of Criticism* (Princeton: Princeton University Press, 1957), p. 187.

15. C. S. Lewis, *An Experiment in Criticism* (Cambridge: Cambridge University Press, 1961), p. 44.

16. W. R. Irwin, "There and Back Again: The Romance of Williams, Lewis, and Tolkien," *Sewanee Review* 69 (Fall 1961): 570–73.

17. Elder Olson, "A Dialogue on Symbolism," R. S. Crane, et al., *Critics and Criticism: Ancient and Modern* (Chicago: University of Chicago Press, 1952), pp. 588–91.

18. Herbert Read, *English Prose Style* (Boston: Beacon Press, Beacon Paperback, 1955), p. 128.

19. C. S. Lewis, ed., *George Macdonald: An Anthology* (New York: Macmillan, 1947), p. 14.

20. Karel Čapek, *In Praise of Newspapers, and Other Essays on the Margin of Literature,* trans. M. and R. Weatherall (London: George Allen and Unwin, 1951), p. 63.

21. C. S. Lewis, *Preface to Paradise Lost* (New York: Oxford University Press, 1942), p. 57.

22. David Foulkes, *The Psychology of Sleep* (New York: Charles Scribner's Sons, 1966), pp. 72–73.

23. C. S. Lewis, *English Literature in the Sixteenth Century, Excluding Drama* (New York: Oxford University Press, 1954), p. 387.

24. J. R. R. Tolkien, "On Fairy-Stories," *Essays Presented to Charles Williams,* ed. C. S. Lewis (New York: Oxford University Press, 1947), p. 67.

25. Amis, op. cit., p. 39.

26. Tolkien, "On Fairy-Stories," p. 76.

27. C. S. Lewis, "Psychoanalysis and Literary Criticism," *They Asked for a Paper: Papers and Addresses* (London: Geoffrey Bles, 1962), pp. 121–23.

28. Edwin Honig, *Dark Conceit: The Making of Allegory* (Evanston: Northwestern University Press, 1959), p. 171.

29. Angus Fletcher, *Allegory: The Theory of a Symbolic Mode* (Ithaca: Cornell University Press, 1964), p. 321.

30. C. S. Lewis, *The Allegory of Love: A Study in Medieval Tradition* (New York: Oxford University Press, 1936), p. 221.

31. C. S. Lewis, "Myth Became Fact," *World Dominion* 22 (Sept.–Oct. 1944): 268–69.

32. J. R. R. Tolkien, "Beowulf: The Monsters and the Critics," *The Proceedings of the British Academy* (New York: Oxford University Press, 1936), 22: 14–15.

33. Walter Allen, *Tradition and Dream: The English and American Novel from the Twenties to Our Time* (London: Phoenix House, 1964), p. 288.

34. Fletcher, op. cit., p. 192.

35. Amis, op. cit., p. 63.

36. Frye, op. cit., p. 117. Frye specifically mentions the stories of Williams and Lewis, which, he remarks, are "largely based on the formulas of the Boy's Own Paper."

37. Lewis, ed., *George Macdonald: An Anthology*, pp. 20–21.

38. Charles Williams, *He Came Down from Heaven*, in *He Came Down from Heaven* and *The Forgiveness of Sins*, 1-vol. ed. (London: Faber & Faber, 1950), p. 70.

39. Tolkien, "On Fairy-Stories," p. 83.

40. *Letters of C. S. Lewis*, ed. W. H. Lewis (New York: Harcourt, Brace & World, 1966), p. 167.

41. Martin Esslin, *The Theatre of the Absurd* (New York: Doubleday, Anchor Books, 1961), pp. 260–61.

42. Lewis, *Preface to Paradise Lost*, p. 89.

43. C. S. Lewis, "Williams and the Arthuriad," *Arthurian Torso*, ed. C. S. Lewis (New York: Oxford University Press, 1948), pp. 101–2.

44. C. S. Lewis, *Rehabilitations and Other Essays* (New York: Oxford University Press, 1939), pp. 191–92.

45. Lewis, *English Literature in the Sixteenth Century, Excluding Drama*, p. 320.

46. Frank Kermode, *The Sense of an Ending: Studies in the Theory of Fiction* (New York: Oxford University Press, 1967), p. 54.

47. Leslie Dewart, *The Future of Belief: Theism in a World Come of Age* (New York: Herder & Herder, 1966), p. 50.

48. C. S. Lewis, *The Discarded Image: An Introduction to Medieval and Renaissance Literature* (Cambridge: Cambridge University Press, 1964), p. 204.

49. This summary is based on Dewart, op. cit., chapter 3.

50. C. S. Lewis, *The Abolition of Man* (New York: Macmillan, 1947), p. 46.

51. Charles Williams, *Witchcraft* (New York: Meridian Books, 1959), p. 311.

52. C. S. Lewis, *Beyond Personality: The Christian Idea of God* (New York: Macmillan, 1945), p. 17.

53. Karl Rahner, S. J., *Nature and Grace: Dilemmas in the Modern Church* (New York: Sheed & Ward, 1964), p. 117.

54. Etienne Gilson, *The Spirit of Medieval Philosophy*, trans. A. H. C. Downes (New York: Charles Scribner's Sons, 1940), pp. 96, 260–61.

55. C. S. Lewis, *Surprised by Joy: The Shape of My Early Life* (New York: Harcourt, Brace & World, 1955), p. 167.

56. Arthur Machen, *Hieroglyphics: A Note upon Ecstasy in Literature* (New York: Knopf, 1923), pp. 139, 160, 163.

57. Charles N. Cochrane, *Christianity and Classical Culture: A Study of Thought and Action from Augustus to Augustine* (New York: Oxford University Press, Galaxy Book, 1957), pp. 430–31.

58. See Dewart, op. cit., pp. 90–91, 192; also his *Foundations of Belief* (New York: Herder & Herder, 1969), p. 255.

59. Rudolf Bultmann, *History and Eschatology: The Presence of Eternity* (New York: Harper & Row, Harper Torchbooks, 1962), p. 44.

60. E. R. Baltazar, "Teilhard de Chardin: A Philosophy of Procession," *New Theology No. 2*, ed. Martin Marty and Dean Peerman (New York: Macmillan, 1965), pp. 139 ff.

61. Dewart, *The Future of Belief*, pp. 195, 190.

62. Ibid., pp. 92, 110.

63. C. S. Lewis, *Miracles: A Preliminary Study* (New York: Macmillan, 1947), p. 185.

64. Dewart, *The Future of Belief*, p. 194.

65. Ibid., pp. 64, 61.

66. Ibid., p. 112.

67. Quoted in Kermode, op. cit., p. 141.

68. Gabriel Marcel, *Homo Viator: Introduction to a Metaphysic of Hope* (Chicago: Henry Regnery Co., 1951), p. 180.

69. Williams, *The Forgiveness of Sins*, p. 164.

70. Charles Williams, "The Way of Affirmation," *The Image of the City and Other Essays*, ed. Anne Ridler (New York: Oxford University Press, 1958), pp. 156–57.

71. John Knox, *Jesus, Lord and Christ* (New York: Harper & Bros., 1958), pp. 229, 235.

72. Williams, "The Cross," *The Image of the City*, p. 138.

73. The sentence (which accurately reflects, I think, Williams' position) is Mary Shideler's, from *The Theology of Romantic Love: A Study in the Writings of Charles Williams* (New York: Harper & Row, 1962), p. 69.

74. Richard R. Niebuhr, *Schleiermacher on Christ and Religion: A New Introduction* (New York: Charles Scribner's Sons, 1964), pp. 163–64.

75. Rahner, op. cit., p. 125.

76. Ibid., pp. 126–27, 133.

77. Ibid., pp. 116, 132.

78. "Tolkien on Tolkien," *Diplomat Magazine* 18 (Oct. 1966): 39.

79. J. R. R. Tolkien, *The Fellowship of the Ring*, p. 52. Subsequent references (by volume and page, in parentheses) will be to the Houghton Mifflin edition (1956), vol. 1: *The Fellowship of the Ring;* vol. 2: *The Two Towers;* vol. 3: *The Return of the King.*

80. Bultmann, op. cit., p. 141.

81. Marcel, op. cit., p. 37.

82. Gilson, op. cit., pp. 163–64.

83. Bultmann, op. cit., p. 94.

84. Ibid., p. 62.

85. Burton Cooper, "The Idea of God: A Whiteheadian Critique of Aquinas' Concept of God" (Th.D. diss. Union Theological Seminary, 1968), p. 189.

86. A few theologians have begun to make the concept of hope—on a model like the one suggested here—the central category for their work; see, especially, Jürgen Moltmann's *Theology of Hope* (New York: Harper & Row, 1967) and *Religion, Revolution, and the Future* (New York: Charles Scribner's Sons, 1969).

87. C. S. Lewis, "On Stories," p. 102.

88. The phrase is Derek Stanford's, in *Christopher Fry: An Appreciation* (London: Peter Nevill, 1951), p. 32. The subject of wonder is explored, lovingly and in depth, in Sam Keen's *Apology for Wonder* (New York: Harper & Row, 1969).

89. Pierre Teilhard de Chardin, *The Future of Man,* trans. Norman Denny (New York: Harper & Row, 1964), p. 236.

90. Ibid., p. 268.

91. Norman O. Brown, *Life Against Death: The Psychoanalytical Meaning of History* (New York: Random House, Vintage Books, 1959), p. 93. See also Herbert Marcuse, *Eros and Civilization* (Boston: Beacon Press, 1955).

92. Robert A. Heinlein, *Stranger in a Strange Land* (New York: G. P. Putnam's Sons, 1961).

93. Austin Farrer, *The Glass of Vision* (London: Dacre Press, 1948), p. 78.

94. Ian T. Ramsey, *Christian Discourse: Some Logical Explorations* (New York: Oxford University Press, 1965), p. 88.

95. Sören Kierkegaard, *The Journals of Sören Kierkegaard,* ed. and trans. Alexander Dru (New York: Oxford University Press, 1938), item 514.

96. Ramsey, *Christian Discourse,* pp. 79, 68, 70.

97. Ibid., pp. 80, 22.

98. John Bayley, *The Characters of Love: A Study in the Literature of Personality* (London: Constable & Co., 1960), p. 34.

99. Dewart, *The Future of Belief,* p. 95.

100. Kermode, op. cit., pp. 38–39, 64, 177.